GOD in the DARK SIDE of CHICAGO

A Story of Pain and Redemption

Brian T. Heath

TEACH Services, Inc.
PUBLISHING
www.TEACHServices.com • (800) 367-1844

World rights reserved. This book or any portion thereof may not be copied or reproduced in any form or manner whatever, except as provided by law, without the written permission of the publisher, except by a reviewer who may quote brief passages in a review.

The author assumes full responsibility for the accuracy of all facts and quotations as cited in this book. The opinions expressed in this book are the author's personal views and interpretations, and do not necessarily reflect those of the publisher. This book is provided with the understanding that the publisher is not engaged in giving spiritual, legal, medical, or other professional advice. If authoritative advice is needed, the reader should seek the counsel of a competent professional.

Copyright Â© 2015 TEACH Services, Inc.
ISBN-13: 978-1-4796-0560-6 (Paperback)
ISBN-13: 978-1-4796-0561-3 (ePub)
ISBN-13: 978-1-4796-0562-0 (Mobi)
Library of Congress Control Number: 2015909066

All scripture quotations, unless otherwise indicated, are taken from the King James Version. Public domain.

Scripture quotations marked NASB are taken from the New American Standard Bible®, Copyright © 1960, 1962, 1963, 1968, 1971, 1972, 1973, 1975, 1977, 1995 by The Lockman Foundation. Used by permission.

Scripture quotations marked TLB are from The Living Bible copyright © 1971 by Tyndale House Foundation. Used by permission of Tyndale House Publishers Inc., Carol Stream, Illinois 60188. All rights reserved.

Scripture quotations marked (NIV) are taken from the Holy Bible, New International Version®, NIV®. Copyright © 1973, 1978, 1984, 2011 by Biblica, Inc.™ Used by permission of Zondervan. All rights reserved worldwide.

Some of the names in this book have been changed to protect the identity and privacy of the individuals.

Dedication

I dedicate this book to the spiritual family that God brought into my life. They have been by my side through good times and bad. When I was sad and discouraged, they were there to pray for me and to encourage me that everything would be all right. They accepted me for who I am and believed in me when I did not always believe in myself. I am so grateful for my spiritual mom, Connie Thompson, and for Aunt Debbie Weiland and Aunt Shirley Dear. I also give thanks for Michael and Miriam Hedges, my pastors Florin Liga and Steve Nelson, and Sister Samantha Nelson.

I also am thankful for Mrs. Tina Wolfe. Having been in prison since I was fifteen years old, I have never had a job, never paid bills, never filed income taxes, and never done a host of other common life tasks. Mrs. Wolfe went out of her way to show me how to do these things.

Praise God for my cute and funny baby sister Ireena Washington, who, though she may not remember me, brought joy into her brother's troubled life. I also thank God for my mother, Yolanda Washington, who gave me life and raised me, as I have concluded, the only way she knew how. She and I will always be a part of each other. Great-Grandma Thea and Grandma Edna, I really do miss you! Last of all, I dedicate this book to my unofficial counselor, teacher, therapist, and friend who fed me with as much knowledge as I could hold, listened to me, spoke the truth to me to keep me in the straight path, and went out of her way to make me a better person. For what each of you have done, I will always be grateful. May God bless you.

Preface

I have been hesitant to allow strangers to know about my life and its long-held secrets, for, once they know, what will they think of me? Will they treat me as they have? Will they look at me with pity or sympathy?

Gaining sympathy is not what I seek. Rather, it is to make people aware of those around them who need to be rescued from situations beyond their control. It is to encourage people to grow beyond the mistakes of their past. If you are a person who was abused, you do not have to pass the abuse on. You can stop the cycle of abuse and not inflict on another the pain that you did not like yourself. If you are a person who has abused, then you must try to understand the pain that you have inflicted. The cycle of abuse can end with you. We can use the pain we have experienced as leverage to help us sympathize with others, or we can dwell on the past and cause our family and friends pain as we seek their sympathy and pity rather than looking to our Creator for help.

Gloomy thoughts of what I need to write cloud my mind. My hand shakes, my chest is tight, my stomach is in a knot, and I feel like I am drowning in fear. I write, not to anger anyone, but only to release the demons of my own anger, pain, misery, and bitterness that have festered inside. The release, I hope, is not for me only, but also for others who have suffered mental, physical, and spiritual abuse. It is also for those who have abused. Like a message in a bottle, hurtful thoughts have floated in me for the past thirty-two years. It is time for the painful message trapped inside to come out. Therefore, with much trepidation, I share with you my story. By God's grace, I survived my ordeal and am wiser and stronger for having lived through it. However, I would like to spare other children the awful experience that was mine. Someone only needs to take the time to demonstrate to them what love really is.

The Bible tells us to forgive, so I am attempting to forgive those who hurt me, and I am hoping that those I have hurt will forgive me as well. It is not reasonable to expect that those who have wronged us will always recognize the pain that they have caused and ask our forgiveness. Many times we must move on without their apologies, forgiving them just the same.

I wrote the poems in this book long after the events, although they are included to help you understand what I remember of my reflections while incarcerated and forecast the events the chapter will describe.

It is my prayer that those who read this book will be touched by it and will be motivated, by God's grace, to help God's children who have suffered abuse.

Contents

Chapter 1	*A Beautiful Mother.*	9
Chapter 2	*A Heart's Soul.*	13
Chapter 3	*A Single Dove, a Sign of Lost Love.*	19
Chapter 4	*Always Been There.*	23
Chapter 5	*Reminiscing.*	31
Chapter 6	*Home Sweet Home.*	37
Chapter 7	*Run, Baby, Run.*	45
Chapter 8	*My Little Angel.*	51
Chapter 9	*Where Were You?.*	57
Chapter 10	*A Lonely Child.*	63
Chapter 11	*True Love.*	69
Chapter 12	*Who Cares?.*	73
Chapter 13	*Questions.*	81
Chapter 14	*While I Am Here Waiting!.*	87
Chapter 15	*A Misguided Child.*	93
Chapter 16	*A Prisoner's Prayer.*	101
Chapter 17	*"Go Read".*	109
Chapter 18	*I Am Free.*	121
Chapter 19	*I Know You Are There.*	126

A Beautiful Mother

A beautiful mother is the one who carried you in her womb until
    she gave you birth, bringing your living soul into this world.

She was there to give you something to ease the pain when your
    first tooth came in, as her sweet mother had done for her.

She was there when you started crawling, and even
    when you started walking. She was there when you
    said "dada" and "mama" for the first time.

She changed your diapers. You were the one who her heart claimed.

She was the one who fed you in the middle of the night, and the
    one who will always love you as long as she has breath.

She was the one who cared for you through chicken pox and
    measles (and protected you from neighborhood weasels).

She watched you stay up when you first biked and was the
    one you pointed out the first person you liked.

She was there when you walked down the aisle for graduation and
    was there with tears in her eyes at your wedding celebration.

When times get lonely and hard, she is the one who is always there
    for you, loving and caring as beautiful mothers always do.

Chapter 1
A Beautiful Mother

"It is to the credit of human nature that except where its selfishness is brought into play, it loves more than it hates. Hatred, by a gradual and quiet process, will even be transformed to love, unless the change be impeded by a continually new irritation of the original feeling of hostility."

– Nathaniel Hawthorne, *The Scarlet Letter*

An inner city teenager sits in the police station, grilled for hours about the murder of a man who lived doors away from his parents' home. How did he get here? What led up to this horrible turn in his life? The story is painful and describes harsh realities of inner city life that many will not likely understand. In the end, the teenager, now a young man, found hope. A blessed surprise of redemption and restoration awaited him. That young man tells his story. May you marvel at God's neverfailing love and goodness for His children!

I was born Brian Tyrone Heath on October 13, 1979, at Louis Weiss Memorial Hospital at 4646 N. Main Drive on the north side of Chicago. My mother and father were Yolanda Heath and David Crowder Sturkey (whose name I didn't know until I was thirty-one years old and whom I only met twice in my life when I was about five years of age). I have an older brother named James Heath whom I saw last when I was around nine. I grew up with my brother Jarmal Heath, who is eight months and two weeks older than I am, owing to my being born two months premature. They referred to us as "Irish twins" because we were born so close together.

My mother was a woman of few words and a giant puzzle. Rarely did she ever utter the words "I love you" to my brother Jarmal or me. Rarely did we even receive a hug. She likely did not know how to express such feelings, though it was easy to tell when she was angry! To this day, I know nothing about her childhood or her teenage years. I do not know her favorite food, her favorite color, her favorite movie – her favorite anything. What I know about her came from other family members. It is not pleasant to hear from others about the skeletons in your mother's closet.

In March of 2008, my great-grandmother Theola Jointer passed away at age ninety-two. I regret that the incarceration from the crime that I will describe in this book kept me from getting much of a chance to talk to her. However, I do remember her telling me once to talk to my cousin Cedrica about my babyhood. What Cedrica told me was a total shock! She said that I was born two months premature and had tubes connected all over my body at the hospital. Since I was so very tiny, my mother was afraid that I was going to die. That reality was too much for her, so she escaped by running away – literally! She ran right out of the hospital, leaving me behind, and did not come back until my Aunt Bonnie made her do so. It is not clear to me how long I was under the hospital's care without her, yet my cousin told me that I lived with Aunt Bonnie until I was about four years old. When I was older and healthy enough, Mom took me home. It is hard to believe that this is true, but it must be true if my great-grandmother told my cousin to tell me. What makes a mother abandon her sick, newborn baby because she gave birth too early? Neither she nor I was to blame for my premature birth, yet I suffered for it.

It took me from 2005 to 2011 to confront my mother about this. Then I was thirty-one. After I confronted her, my cousin told me about another incident that took place when I was eight or nine months old. I got sick with parasitic worms and would not stop crying. My cousin said that my mother said that I was possessed with demons and she locked me in a treasure trunk, putting it out on the back porch. I do not know how long I stayed there, but my cousin told me that Aunt Bonnie found me and took me home with her. Once again, I do not know how true the story is, but my great-grandmother wanted me to know it. To hear it was definitely unsettling, and it threw fuel on what was by then a massive fire inside me.

When I confronted my mother, she got very defensive and denied every bit of it. She told me that I never lived with Aunt Bonnie, and she denied the story of the treasure trunk, saying that a person has to have treasure to own a treasure chest, as if I did not know that people use trunks to store clothes. Her explanation was not convincing. With her whole life a mystery to me, I could not take my mother's word over the word of my great-grandmother and cousin, though I would have liked to. In the end, I believed what they told me. However, though they meant well, I don't think they knew the damage they were doing by telling me those things. It is

Chapter 1 *A Beautiful Mother*

sometimes better to leave sleeping dogs lie. Yet, I accept my great-grandmother's genuine concern that I know the truth about my very early life and my mother's actions, even though what I learned is confusing to me. Asking why is not always helpful, even though things generally do happen for a reason.

I was twenty-five the last time I spoke with my great-grandmother. Her last words were: "You've overcome a lot, and you can overcome anything. Always pray and never give up. I love you." I never heard her voice again, but I will never forget her words.

A Heart's Soul

A heart's soul is a very passionate and caring desire.
    It's a candle that glows and pierces the darkest
    of many nights, setting your soul on fire.

A heart's soul is not soft as water, but is harder than concrete.
    It will climb the highest mountain and wait
    on the moon and stars to meet.

A heart's soul is the rushing water of the beautiful river.
    It is the sound of thunder that can make you quiver.

A heart's soul is very determined to give you all the emotion you
    feel. It is the sleepy sound of rain falling against your windowsill.

A heart's soul is the only reason for our existence on this
    planet. It is quiet and swift, so pray and don't miss it.
    Make sure you open up your heart to catch it.

A heart's soul is the Holy Spirit who is always there for you
    when everything's going wrong, and you start feeling blue.

A heart's soul is always there no matter how old you are.
    It will be right by your side and not very far.

Chapter 2
A Heart's Soul

"Love is too large, too deep ever to be truly understood or measured or limited within the framework of words."

– Dr. Scott Peck, *The Road Less Traveled*

My family and I used to live at 4540 N. Magnolia on the north side of Chicago in a huge, worn-down apartment complex. The area was pretty much a ghetto. Our apartment building was between two vacant lots. A good friend of my mother owned the building. Any time I said the word "white" as a racial reference, she used to tell me: "She's not white; she's a hillbilly." At age four, I didn't understand what she meant. In our neighborhood, there were a number of "hillbillies," as she called them. Among them there were "Jugheads" and "Bubbas," just like there were "Charlies" and "Joes" among the blacks. They were good people, although, at such a young age, I couldn't understand why so many of them seemed to always walk around barefooted, drinking Mad Dog 20/20, and eating mud-clay sandwiches between two pieces of bread. What I remember most about the "hillbillies" is that they were very protective of the children in the neighborhood and that they allowed nothing to happen to us.

I went to Stockton Preschool, and I especially recall my graduation day. We kids were all happy because we were about to start kindergarten. My mother had dressed up my brother and me, and she let me wear one of her gold chains. While we were at the school party, a little girl walked up to me, while I stood by shyly smiling, and she told me that she liked me! At four years of age, I did not really understand what was going on, but I do remember her asking me to be her boyfriend. I was happy to accept her request because I thought that being a boyfriend meant just carrying your girlfriend's lunch, holding her hand, and giving her something from your lunch if she wanted it. Not twenty minutes later, she asked me if she could have my gold chain.

I didn't realize that my mother was only letting me borrow the chain. At that age, I thought that anything I saw or touched was mine, no matter what it was.

When she asked me for the chain, I told her, "This is my only chain."

She responded, "And you are my only boyfriend."

I retorted, "This is my first chain."

She shot back, "You are my first boyfriend."

That little girl was so quick on her toes that I thought that giving her the chain must be the right thing to do. Dryly I said, "I guess you can have it then," and I took the chain from around my neck and gave it to her. She smiled at me, gave me a kiss on my cheek and skipped off while I stood there, rocking back and forth, with my hands in my pockets and a big "Kool-aid" smile on my face.

After a while, I went back to where my mother and brother were standing and was feeling all happy and giggly. It was time to take our individual and class pictures. All of a sudden, my mother realized that my chain was missing, and she asked me where it was. I told her I had given it to my girlfriend, and she gasped, "Girlfriend? You did what?"

I repeated what I had done, feeling very proud of myself, "I gave it to my girlfriend."

Then, she said to me very clearly, with her expression changing quickly from shock to anger, "You need to go get it back from your girlfriend!"

My brother Jarmal, who was standing next to my mother, didn't make matters any better when he let out that two-tone sound that children make when someone else has gotten in trouble, "uh-ohhhh," but Mom just held her composure and told me to just get it back.

I ran around looking for my new girlfriend of less than an hour who had already gotten me in trouble. However, for some reason, I could not find her. I looked everywhere, but I could not find her. I went back to my mother and told her that I could not find the girl. My mother demanded that I keep looking. As I continued to look, I noticed that everyone was beginning to have cookies and juice, but, since I was busy looking for a little con artist who had tricked me out of my chain, I was missing out. After a while, I got tired of looking for her, went over to a corner, and stood with my arms crossed, biting my lower lip and trying not to cry. Then, suddenly, I saw her! She had been hiding behind her mother's skirts, watching me the whole time.

By now, I was so angry and frustrated that I didn't even care about her being my girlfriend. All I could think about was how I would get the chain back. I also remembered how, just a few days before, I had gotten into trouble for giving my brother something and then taking it back, and here I was doing it again. I remembered how Mom had yelled at me: "Don't be an Indian giver!" So, how would I solve this dilemma at four years of age? I was already in trouble and didn't want to be in trouble again for being an "Indian giver." More than that, I didn't want to break up with my first girlfriend or have her calling me an "Indian giver," so I decided to let my "girlfriend" keep the

Chapter 2   A Heart's Soul

chain and just deal with being in trouble with my mother.

After a while, I went back and told my mother that I couldn't find the girl, when I had actually seen her a couple more times before the graduation party was over. I was very relieved when we all went home and my mother just chalked up the chain to a loss. However, the memory of what happened still lives on in me.

As a small child, I was very trusting of other people, and I hated seeing people hurt. Being caring and overly trusting would end up costing me later on in life. Little children don't see people as con artists, pedophiles, or monsters. They don't judge people by the color of their skin, but they do notice things like deformities in the body or missing limbs. Children grow up learning from their surroundings, such as what their parents do and the people with whom they associate. At times, they learn from the mistakes they make. Without proper guidance, I just seemed to keep making mistake after mistake.

I recall learning in first grade that what I thought was having fun and getting along with my classmates was considered disruption of the class, and I was quickly labeled a class clown. My teacher must have asked me at least ten times to sit down, calm down, and stop disrupting the class, but I didn't hear her and didn't stop. I was hungry for attention, and I was feeding off my classmates' laughter, so I just kept going until our poor teacher could take it no longer. She came over, grabbed me out of my chair, and plunked me down in a small chair in the corner, shaking her finger in my face and commanding, "Now you stay right here and be quiet!" Her actions put me in a panic, and I grabbed the little chair and threw it at her. Then I charged at her full speed, hitting her in the legs, kicking her, biting her, and tearing a hole in her stockings. What I did was in misguided self-protection. I wound up being suspended for a couple of days.

That afternoon when I got home I got in trouble with my parents, although I don't remember exactly what my punishment was. I know that it included not being able to watch television or go outside. When Mom asked me why I had attacked the teacher, I told her that it was because she had told me to not ever let anybody touch me – especially a stranger, and to bite, kick, hit, and scream to defend myself. So, that is what I did. Anybody who wasn't related to me I considered a stranger. As a kid, I believed every word my parents said, no matter what it was. I admired and idolized my parents and wanted to be like them, to talk like them, to dress like them, and to be grown up.

In my youth, my mouth got me into trouble quite frequently. My mother never tried to watch her language in front of us kids, and we consumed her words like a person eating a banana split. Then, when the adults were not around, we would curse like the adults with each other. I can remember when my cursing got me in trouble.

One day my mother was cooking something and needed some sugar that she must have thought she had but couldn't find. She said, "What happened to the blankety-blank shuga?" Since I didn't know what had happened to it, I answered, "I don't know what happened to the blankety-blank shuga, Mama." She turned to face me and gave me that look that said, "You done messed up, child!" I bolted out of the kitchen to get out of her reach.

Then, another day, we were sitting on our neighbors' porch across the street from our house, and my mother was wearing red pump heels, and she looked at her heels and noticed that something had chewed on them. She pulled off the shoe, looked at it, and said, "Who 'blanked' up my heel?" You can pretty much guess what my response to her remark was. "I ain't 'blanked' up your heel, Mama." Yes, I got that look again. But the thing was, we didn't have a dog or a puppy to chew on her heel, and our cat didn't do it, even though we had a cat that was so huge it had a head like a dog, which we named "Dog." We guessed that it must have been mice that chewed on her shoe, and the pests in our apartment are the reason I hate bugs to this day.

Ours was a small, shabby apartment with just one room. The living room served as a bedroom for my mother and her boyfriend "Tricky," whose real name was Thomas. There was a small kitchen to the right, and to the left and through the doorway, a room that was more like a closet, though it was big enough for a twin-sized bed. That was where my brother and I slept. The bathroom was directly across from "the closet," and a clothesline hung just above our bed. Talk about small! It was much smaller than the apartments in the housing projects.

One day my mother put us to bed earlier than usual because she was having a couple of friends over. I remember the thick smell of cigarette smoke and alcohol on such occasions. At first, it was too dark for my brother and me to see in our "closet" bedroom. However, after awhile, we got adjusted to the dark. I looked around our room and saw a dark-looking thing on the wall. "Look at that!" I said. For some reason, my brother always slept with a flashlight, and he took it and shined it on the thing on the wall. It was a cockroach the size of a man's thumb. I didn't know that roaches were nocturnal. Apparently, the creature hated the light, and it buzzed as it flew away. It reminded me of the monster in "Jeepers Creepers" and it certainly gave me the creeps. That experience was when I realized how fast I could run. I tore out of the room, not looking back at that fearful flying thing! Overcome by our imaginations, Jarmal and I jumped on our big wheels and tried to get away from it, exiting our apartment and peddling down the long hallway that led outside. I felt a bit relieved, as we peddled down the block away from our apartment building and the plastic wheels of our Big Wheels ground the grit of the sidewalk. Ever after, I was afraid of insects.

When we returned to our apartment, my mother had not been aware of our absence or of how scared we had been. She and her company were engrossed in laughter and music, and the little apartment reeked with stale cigarette smoke. No one in the party paid any attention to us as we stood watching their activities. The excitement had had an effect on both

Chapter 2 *A Heart's Soul*

my brother and me, and we headed to the bathroom. However, my brother beat me inside. In agony, I waited something like twenty minutes outside the bathroom, banging and kicking on the door. That only made things worse. After another fifteen minutes, I could hold it no longer, and I messed my pants and the hallway floor. When my mother walked in and saw the mess on the floor, she asked what it was. I said, "The cat did it." My cover was almost believable, if you knew what our cat was capable of doing. However, I really don't think my mom believed me. She probably was too embarrassed to discipline me, so she went along with my story. After cleaning the floor and myself, I still had to go back into the little bedroom of which I was so afraid.

My mother, at this time, drank a lot. She was not a "sloppy drunk," nevertheless, she was a drunk. However, she kept us fed and kept up her daily tasks. I don't remember her hugging me or showing me affection. Though she tried to show her love to us in her own way, I really don't think she knew how.

My mom's boyfriend Thomas, or "Tricky," was an Army veteran. I don't recall him yelling at us or hitting us, but he loved to drink. He used to say to us, "Don't drink this stuff; it will kill you." That's the only thing he said that I remember. One day he just wasn't at the apartment anymore. Later we found out that he had died of cirrhosis of the liver.

When, at Thomas's funeral, the men in uniform gave my mother a folded American flag, she cried, which was the first time I remember seeing her cry. As I got older, I would periodically look at his picture from the funeral to try to remember him, but I couldn't. All I could remember was what he had told me about never touching alcohol. I do remember that, in life, he looked like Lamont on the television show *Sanford and Son*.

Thomas had one friend whom everybody called "Rodent." He was at Thomas's funeral. It was not long after the funeral that my family saw more and more of him at our house, and our life took a dramatic turn.

A Single Dove,
a Sign of Lost Love

As I look out my window to the world's most beautiful sky,
    My wandering eye catches a single dove passing by.

I wonder if it's searching for its mate.
    Guided by love and not what one may call "fate."

Hour by hour the dove flies on this hot and stifling day,
    Is he speaking to my heart in a supernatural way?

I wonder why the dove hovers so steadily over me,
    Do we link together by something no one else can see?

I search my heart as I review the cloudy sky above,
    The dove is gone. I hope he's found his missing love.

Chapter 3
A Single Dove, a Sign of Lost Love

"All true love is unconditional. Once it becomes conditional, it is not true love, but a subtle attempt to control, manipulate, change, or gain power over others or another."

– Sal Baba

Rodent started hanging around my mother, and we saw more and more of him, crossing paths in the oddest of places. One day when Mom, Jarmal, and I were in a grocery store, there he was – 220 pounds, six feet tall, bald headed and goateed, with a dark chocolate complexion. He was at the store with his girlfriend, Nancy, a white girl. He and she got into an argument because Nancy, who did not know how to cook, had come back to meet him with bologna lunchmeat in her hands, rather than the meat he had asked her to buy, and Rodent came walking with a loaf of white bread in his. Upset, Rodent swung the bread at Nancy and hit her in the head. The bread went everywhere, and she ran out of the store. That was the last time I ever saw Nancy, and that is when Rodent found his lost love because my mother was a very good cook.

No more bologna sandwiches, hot dogs, or Spaghetti-Os for Rodent. My mother could cook him steak and potatoes, capturing his heart through his stomach.

But there was trouble from the start. The first thing was that he hated cats, and our cat, named "Dog," used to lick his feet when he was asleep. One day Rodent got his revenge. He waited until Dog walked by the window – a fifth story window – and then he kicked him out of it. From that day on, we never had another cat, and Dog never returned. We did get a dog, after a while – a German Shepherd we named "Killer." Unfortunately, our apartment was too small for such a huge dog and a confrontation was bound to take place. It happened the day that Mom was cooking smothered potatoes with T-bone steak and Rodent was eating his meal on a TV tray. Killer walked by and, seeing his opportunity, grabbed the steak and took off running, with Rodent right behind him with a butcher knife, ready to kill Killer. Rodent was so mad that he flipped my mother's sleeper sofa bed over with one hand and chased Killer around the apartment until my mother opened the front door and gave Killer a way of escape, which he gladly took. He flew out of the apartment and down the hallway with Jarmal and I yelling behind him, "Goodbye, Killer." We never saw Killer again; nor did we have any pets for a couple years.

I think the first movie that my family watched together was *Charlotte's Web* – a movie about Wilbur the pig. The plot of the movie is about how Wilber the pig avoids being slaughtered. It just so happened that our dinner that night was pork chops! Jarmal and I reacted, yelling, "They killed Wilbur!" At that moment, we vowed to never eat pork again. Rodent didn't care how we felt, and he said, "Good, then – more for me!" My mother thought that this was cute, but, because of Rodent, she didn't change her dinner plans. Now, if we weren't going to eat the pork, all that was left in the meal were vegetables. Not being used to such, you can understand why our vow to never eat pork again was short-lived and lasted only about two weeks.

I can remember the first time I got a whipping from Rodent. My brother and I were outside playing in a vacant lot, and my brother threw a rock pretty far. Since he was my older brother, I wanted to be just like him, so I tried to throw a rock as far as he did, but I couldn't. He must have thrown his rock twenty-five to thirty yards. Putting everything I had into it, I threw my rock and it went flying on and on. I watched it and thought, *Yeah, I beat you*. However, my rock did not go beyond twenty yards. I had just thrown it high up into the air. When it came down, it hit a kid. Ow! I didn't mean to do that. I wish I could have taken that moment back. The kid's calm response was remarkable. He acted like nothing was bothering him, but, the whole time, he was collecting smooth, slick rocks. He then moved in a little, about fifteen yards, and unleashed a fury of rocks on us. I heard the first one zip past my head, and I took off running and hid behind a car. The second rock hit my brother dead square under his eye, and blood went everywhere as it split his skin wide open. Jarmal hit the ground screaming, then he got up and ran into the house. I ran after him.

After everything calmed down, Jarmal told Rodent and my mother what had happened, and Rodent grabbed a belt and whipped me for throwing that rock – a total accident – and for not going after that kid and beating him up. How tough was a five-year-old kid supposed to be? Rodent told my mother that he was going to toughen us up, but what he really ended up doing was creating a little monster full of hatred.

A couple months passed; I don't know how many whippings I had received. Yet, the next scene I remember was when my mother, Jarmal, and I were going to the liquor store across the street. By now, Jarmal was bullying me, his little brother. I suppose an older sibling bully-

Chapter 3 *A Single Dove, a Sign of Lost Love*

ing a younger sibling could be considered normal. However, Jarmal crossed the line, and I paid for it. As we crossed the street and got to the curb, Jarmal pushed me in my back, and I went hands first into the dirt, where there were broken bottles. I cut my left palm about an inch deep and about two inches long. I cried my eyes out, and my mother wrapped my hand up in my T-shirt and walked me around the corner to the fire station. The firemen took me by ambulance to Weiss Hospital. The nurse there worked on me, calming me down and cleaning my wound with brown iodine and a sponge. I noticed a rubber brush on the other side of the sponge. Then came "Dr. Evil"! It really seemed that he must have hated kids and that he was taking out his feelings on me and my hand! He took the sponge from the nurse and flipped it over. Immediately a look of shock came over my face, and I knew that I was about to experience a whole lot of pain. He took the rubber brush and scrubbed my hand like it was a gym shoe, and I kept yelling and trying to get away, kicking, screaming, whatever it took to end the torture. (How is a small kid supposed to know that such a wound, if not properly cleaned, could be disastrous?) What lasted about a minute seemed like an eternity. He finally stitched me up and sent me home. Though I was completely exhausted from what could have been my death, my mother still had to stop on our way home in her olive-tan Nova to pick up her liquor.

When we got to the apartment, Rodent asked what had happened, and my mother told him that I had fallen. I said loud and clear, "He pushed me!" My mother and stepfather just ignored me, as if I hadn't said anything, and Jarmal never got into trouble over it. It was at that moment that I realized that there was favoritism in my home, and the rules that applied to me didn't apply to Jarmal.

Always Been There

Ever since I could remember, I felt You calling me to You,
    I was so young and unaware, what was I supposed to do?

I knew You were watching and guarding me.
    Yet, I didn't understand what You wanted me to be.

When times were hard, and I didn't look to You,
    it was because no one taught me to.

I looked for someone to shelter me from the monsters of the street,
    when my Father above cared for me, no one could dare compete.

I am grateful that You are loving, patient, forgiving, and kind.
    After the life I've lived, tender love is hard to find.

There were times, I bowed down and went to You in prayer,
    now I know it's true that You've always been there!

Chapter 4
Always Been There

"Angels of glory, that do always behold the face of the Father in heaven, joy in ministering to His little ones. Trembling souls, who have many objectionable traits of character, are their special charge. Angels are ever present where they are most needed, with those who have the hardest battle with self to fight, and whose surroundings are the most discouraging. And in this ministry Christ's true followers will co-operate.

– Ellen G. White, *The Desire of Ages*

After moving to Sunnyside, we used to get in the car and just drive. One Saturday when we were driving around we came across a church with the sign "Seventh-day Adventist" outside. Puzzled to see people going to church on a different day than we went to church, I asked my mother who the Seventh-day Adventists were, and she said they were Christians who went to church on Saturday. That didn't make sense to me. It wasn't until after I grew up that I discovered the biblical reasons they didn't go to church on Sunday like we Baptists did. My mother didn't like change, and she didn't want to change from Sunday to Saturday worship. However, she always believed Saturday to be the biblical Sabbath. Yet, she stuck with the Baptist Church because her mother and grandmother were Baptists. That was the family church, and it was the church I had to attend. However, this wouldn't be the last time I crossed paths with the Seventh-day Adventists.

We went to New St. Peter's Baptist Church on the west side of Chicago at 4158 West Chicago Avenue. Uncle Walter Crockran was the pastor. He was a big man with a powerful voice. I was about seven years old by then, and I used to have overwhelming feelings of being drawn to church. Mom never taught us about God, yet I kept getting strong feelings of an unseen Presence that would pull me to church. When I was able to go outside and walk around, I used to stare at a huge church on the corner of Broadway. Many Saturdays I would go inside and sit in the back row and listen to an Asian man preach. Of course, I could not understand him. One day he saw me and started speaking to me in English about how Jesus loved everyone. I really didn't understand the strong feelings that drew me to God's house, yet, I knew that I felt peace, calmness, and safety when I was there. God was touching my young heart.

Unfortunately, I still did foolish things as a child. One day when I walked out of the church, my childish ways took over. As I was sitting at the top of the church steps, I saw a ten – to twelve-year-old kid holding a wire coat hanger and going up and down the street popping open parking meters and stealing quarters. After that I saw him cross the street to a store where he played video games. I wanted to play video games too, so I tried doing what he had done. It didn't work because I didn't have a wire coat hanger. The kid had to be really bad at the video games because he came back just thirty minutes later. This time he showed me how to open the parking meters.

About twenty minutes later, I cracked open my first parking meter, took the quarters out, and went back across the street to play "Centipede" while the other kid played something else. I was so short at the time that I barely reached the controls. I gave the kid four quarters that I had retrieved, and I kept two quarters for myself. Soon I was his little errand boy. He sent me out for more quarters. The first parking meter that I opened had no quarters. The fifth meter had three quarters and a little surprise – the police, who caught me robbing the meter. I don't know whether they filed a police report, but they took me home. I knew it was useless to explain myself or blame someone else because I also knew that I would be whipped or punished a second time. As soon as I got off punishment, I went back to that church a couple more times. Back then, I didn't know what I was looking for; I only knew that I felt peace and safety there.

We stayed at that apartment for about two years, as I recall, but I don't have too many memories of people or the apartment itself. I do remember that we were living there when my mother went back to school and got her first job. I remember that because we were often stuck at home with Rodent and his friend Shadow, who was a big, muscular guy. They told many stories about their days as part of a gang called "Conservative Vice Lords." Rodent was no longer a part of the gang, but Shadow was. Shadow used to call us "little lords." We idolized him, and soon we were calling him "uncle." That is how Jarmal and I got connected with the "CVL" gangs.

During this time, Rodent bought Jarmal a brand new, black and gray BMX bike. I never understood why Jarmal always got the good stuff while I always got hand-me-downs or nothing at all. Of course, he was my older brother, and thankfully he was generous and shared his bike with me. After he mastered riding

Chapter 4 *Always Been There*

without training wheels, he taught me how to ride the bike. I thought I had mastered riding, so he let me go. I started peddling faster and faster to feel the breeze against my face. Then I hit an unseen bump and went flying through the air into a tree. I wasn't hurt, but I was angry that I had dented his front wheel. I was also scared because I knew that I would receive one of Rodent's whippings. Mercifully, Jarmal didn't let that happen. He said to me, "It's OK. It's your bike too. I'll just tell Mama and Rodent that I ran into a tree." Jarmal kept his promise, and – no surprise – he didn't get into any trouble. Mom and Rodent just took the wheel to the store and got a replacement.

One day Jarmal got into a fight and I ran home to get Rodent, but I got a whipping for not staying to help fight. But I wasn't a fighter. Rodent continued his plan to toughen me up since I was a little "scaredy-cat." Down the street from our place was a field house at a park where kids learned to box. One time when I was there, the coach put me in the ring with another kid and put a padded helmet on both of us. I kept telling the coach that I didn't want to fight, but he kept on insisting that I did. Though the kid was about my height, he must have been at least three times bigger than I was. He chased me around the ring, taunting and threatening me. I was afraid. Finally, he charged at me, and, out of pure fear, I brought my hand back and hit him in the nose. He immediately hit the mat, then got up and ran to the washroom. I followed him and heard him crying as he washed away the blood rushing from his nose. I stood there rubbing his back, apologizing, telling him that I didn't want to fight but that they had forced me. That whole week I felt terrible for the kid. I went back to the field house a couple more times, looking for the boy, but I never saw him again to be able to make up for what I had done to him.

Rodent didn't have much luck toughening me up at first. I was compassionate by nature. I never wanted to hurt people. I never wanted to see people get hurt. But over the years the people in my life who wanted to "toughen" me up took my compassion away from me. That's a crime. A person should never do that to a child. They wanted me to be tough, but it only made me more scared and, in time, made me quit caring.

I had another older brother named James. I noticed one day, when my mother saw him, she was happier than I had ever seen her before. Her happiness was like that of the father in the story of the prodigal son when the son returned home. The father was so happy to see him that he ran joyfully to meet him and gave him a big welcome back party. Knowing that we were going where James lived to pick him up, my mother, Rodent, Jarmal, and I got ready. We drove to where he lived on the west side of Chicago. When we got there and I saw him come out of his house, I could see that he had to be my brother. We looked very much alike! I had always heard that James and I had different fathers, while Jarmal and I were supposed to have the same father. Yet, Jarmal and I looked nothing alike. How could I believe what I had heard?

When James got into the car, I was excited to finally see and meet him. However, he acted like Jarmal – I didn't exist. He probably said no more than five words to us, his brothers, the whole time we were in the car together. When he talked, it was to Rodent and my mother.

We ended up going to a strip mall that people called "Jew Town," on Chicago's west side. It had a store where James tried on coats. Mom finally bought him the one he wanted – a Chicago Bears starter coat. That really upset Jarmal and me. We had been trying for months to get Mom and Rodent to buy us that same coat! We never got one, but here they were buying one for James!

That night James spent time with the family, and Jarmal and I tried to talk to him and get to know him, but he wasn't interested. He seemed only interested in getting what he wanted, and in the morning he was gone. I hated him.

I remember that my Grandmother Edna lived just a block from us, and Jarmal and I used to go over and spend the night at her apartment. We enjoyed when she would sit on the floor with us and tell us stories while she drank beer. Even at that age, we recognized that she was intoxicated, but it sure made her stories funnier and more exciting.

One time when we had our first family get-together, Rodent, mom, Grandma Edna, Jarmal, and I went to the Rosemont Horizon to watch a World Wrestling Federation match. Jarmal was a huge wrestling fan, and we watched Hulk Hogan, the Giant, the Legion of Doom, Ultimate Warrior, and many other wrestlers. It was one of the best times we ever had, but I knew in my heart that the trip was really for Jarmal.

A couple of months later, Rodent decided it was time to change his life. He cut back on his drinking, though he still smoked marijuana, and he no longer participated in violent gang activity. He went to church and became a Freemason, but his perspective on raising children was still lacking. He was still abusive, though it was more restrained. However, I noticed that the older we got, the more severe the whippings got. My mother was working, but she drank a lot when she came home. Her drinks of choice were beer and Bacardi. One day her drinking almost got us all killed.

Rodent used to tell my mother to stay away from her friend Lulu. I didn't understand why he would say that, but I had noticed that my mother lost many of her friends when she and Rodent became a couple. On one particular day, I remember taking a walk with my mother, Lulu, and Jarmal. I don't remember why we were walking, and it seemed like we were walking forever. However, soon I had to use the bathroom – urgently – and I told my mother at least twenty times how badly I had to go. Yet, my cry fell on deaf ears, and Lulu told me to "go over there," meaning behind the bushes by someone's house. However, I didn't want to do that. Then Lulu and my mother got into an argument that stopped our progress entirely. I couldn't hold it any longer, so I did as Lulu had suggested and went behind a shrub to take care of my business. There was no sense of propriety in

Chapter 4 *Always Been There*

the matter, Mom wasn't taking me to a public restroom, and I had to go! My apologies to the shrubs and the family who owned them.

That same day we ended up in my mother's car with my mother driving. I was sitting right behind her. Lulu was in the passenger seat, and Jarmal was right behind her. Mom and Lulu were mixing their alcoholic beverages with soda, and they were getting drunker and drunker. Then, out of nowhere, *CRASH*! We slammed into the back of a parked flatbed truck. My brother and I were thrown around in the back seat. We started crying and sobbed, "Mama! Mama!" She didn't answer. Lulu was crying too, and her lip was split open and bleeding badly. Jarmal and I just sat there yelling and crying, with thirty cars or so driving by without stopping to help. Finally, a black car on the other side of the road stopped, and a Hispanic man in a tuxedo with a white coat got out of a car full of other Hispanic people. He pulled my brother and I out of the car. He also called an ambulance and stayed with us until the ambulance arrived. My mother was still not responding much. We went to the hospital, and the nurses checked us over to make sure we were all right. Then Rodent arrived at the hospital, and a nursing assistant wheeled my mother out. She was drowsy and had thrown up all over herself. Neither she nor Rodent seemed concerned about how we were doing. Yet, God was concerned, and He had cradled us in His arms and had protected us from harm.

That winter – just a couple of months later – Rodent joined the church choir. He had a raspy voice that cracked a lot when he sang. To soften up his vocal chords, he would drink salty lemon juice. I tried it one day, and I liked it so much that I asked him for fifty cents so I could buy a lemon at the store. He answered, "No." When my mother came home, I asked her for the money, and she said to wait until Rodent left. When he did, she found her purse and took out fifty cents for Jarmal and me to buy a lemon. I was so happy with her gift that I darted right out of the house and into the street. However, in my haste, I forgot to look both ways and – *WHUNK* – I got hit by a car! I flew into the air and came down between two parked cars. I heard Jarmal calling me, but I couldn't move my legs. I pulled myself up to the curb and told him, "Go get Mama!" Then I laid there hurt. I watched my mother coming out of the house, and I saw the fear on her face. This was the mother I had been looking for! She talked gently to me, told me everything was going to be all right, held my hand, and never left my side. That was the first time I had ever seen her show emotion toward me. I knew then, if I never knew it before, that she really did care for me. I felt more love in that moment than I would feel again for a long time.

The ambulance arrived and took me to the hospital, and I kept asking my mother about the fifty cents. She said, "Don't worry about your fifty cents. Just get better, child." It was hard for me to get it out of my head. We didn't get money very often. Fifty cents was a lot to me.

To shut me up about the fifty cents and the lemon, the nurse said to me,

"I have something for you that is much better than a lemon." Then she gave me a piece of pizza! The doctor let me go home, and I healed without problem. Once again, God had protected me from death. I didn't even have a broken bone!

My next remembrance was when my best friend moved into the house. His arrival was so special that I remember the date. It was February 14, 1988. My new best friend was a pearl-white toy poodle that Rodent bought for my mother, which she named "Butt-Butt." For the first couple of days, the little dog seemed scared to death. However, in a very short while, she warmed up to me. That is my last memory while we lived on the north side of Chicago. That same year we moved to the far south side of Chicago.

Reminiscing

Reminiscing! On being little kids –
    we never paid attention to all the crazy things we did.

Reminiscing! On all the fun times we would have –
    how we'd get together in the basement and crack jokes and laugh!

Reminiscing! On running through the rain –
    when your brothers came to check on me
    when I was beaten and in pain.

Reminiscing! On when you heard I was caught and put in jail,
    and you came up with money for the bail!

Reminiscing! When I received the horrible news of your brothers' death,
    and I fell to my knees unable to catch my breath.

Reminiscing! On how we walked to school, brothers and best friends,
    my love for the two of you won't ever come to an end.

Reminiscing! On how time after time we ran from the police –
    my brothers, you don't have to run anymore;
    you can finally rest in peace.

Reminiscing! When you told me how we'd grow up and succeed,
    now that you are in the sleep of death, my heart will always bleed.

Reminiscing! How I saw your face come back to me in my own reflection,
    now I pray that I will see you in the great resurrection!

Reminiscing! At school in 1988, I first met the group of seven,
    I pray that one day we will meet in heaven.

Reminiscing! You, my friends and brothers, shall never be forgotten.
    I will see you later, Ahmad Barrett and Demar Buffin.

Chapter 5
Reminiscing

"Youth is quick in feeling, but weak in judgment."

– Homer

In the spring of 1988, my family moved to 10718 S. Prairie. When we arrived, it was already night, and the old house seemed dark and creepy. Like the houses in scary movies, the door creaked and the floors squeaked. Every room of that two-story flat was painted green. It had an attic and a basement as well. Next door was a red one-story flat with a torn down garage. I don't remember who lived there first, but, six months after we got there, whoever it was moved out, and the Jeffersons moved in.

Even still, the house was a lot better than the apartment we had been living in. Jarmal and I had our own room. The house had a living room, a dining room, an attic, a basement, and a front and back yard. I hoped that the house would make us more of a family. Though things in our family weren't always so bad, there was no affection toward us kids, stunting our emotional growth.

After a few days, Jarmal and I enrolled at Alfred D. Kohn Elementary School. That is where I met Ahmad Barrett and Demar Buffin. Demar didn't attend school at Kohn, so I wondered how he happened to be there that day. The big difference between that school and the one I had attended before were the gangs in this school. It seemed like everybody was part of a gang. That may seem strange to you if you didn't grow up in the inner city. Being part of a gang was the norm and how kids banded together to protect themselves. When other kids asked me what group I belonged to, without hesitation I told them, "I'm a Conservative Vice Lord," not really understanding what it could cost me. Demar and Ahmad were Four Corner Hustlers, and the rest of the school were Gangster Disciples. Being outsiders made us something like brothers. We needed to stick together against our common enemy.

Kohn School had two buildings – a smaller building for kindergarten through 6th grade, and the bigger building for 7th and 8th grade. I didn't understand how Jarmal was in Cone class, and I was in another class in that same little building, but just that separation in the same building, although we were in the same grade, made me a target. I was chased home from school daily and was an easy target because we were let out at a different time, and I was always by myself when school let out. Jarmal, Demar, Ahmad, and a few other friends were always together and looked out for each other.

I remember the day that I was caught while being chased home from school. The boys were chasing me with golf clubs and swinging them at me. Despite my speed, someone tripped me that day. By the grace of God, the police showed up just then out of nowhere! I was never so happy to see them. It is, after all, their job "to protect and to serve." If it weren't for the police, those boys could have beaten me to death. Yet, that was not in God's plan. While the police made the other kids go away, my brother came running up the street with five other boys. The police searched him and found a pair of homemade *nunchaku* on him. Apparently he planned to use them, fancying himself as Bruce Lee! That is the problem with watching too many karate movies. Five years in that school were a daily torture.

One day I was suspended for five days for fighting. I came home from school and had to explain to Rodent about my suspension and the gang violence. However, he didn't want to hear it. He just brought out the extension cord and beat me with it for at least ten minutes. Every day that I wasn't in school I got beaten with the extension cord and had to clean the house. I also had restrictions on watching television and being able to go outside. It is true that I was in a gang, but I didn't seek out any of the fights that were happening daily. I finally figured out that it was easier to fight outside the school, and Demar and Ahmad and my new friend Kelvin would try to console me afterward, but it didn't work.

During my grammar school years, Derrick and Craig Hardaway, who were later convicted of killing a boy named "Yummy," bullied me day and night. After dealing with their bullying every day, I would have to come home and deal with Rodent as well. My mother didn't try to stop him. She just kept her mouth closed and let the beatings happen because Rodent was the man of the house. I hated living there, and I hated Rodent that much more with each additional beating.

I remember an incident in math class, when a girl kept teasing me about my clothes, saying things like "Why don't you wear good name brands like Jarmal?" and kept calling me names like "Stinky" and "Ugly," so I insulted her with one of the abusive words I had learned from the adults. After school I was walking by myself when that same girl called me. As I turned around, she slapped me! I didn't want to hit a girl, but she kept swinging and swinging at me until I finally punched her in the eye. The next thing I knew, ten girls were beating me up! I just couldn't

Chapter 5   *Reminiscing*

win at that school. I hated it! My friends tried to protect me, but always arrived after I had been beaten up. I knew Rodent knew about these daily fights at school, but he didn't care.

The next day I went back to school and tried to apologize to the girl for hitting her in the eye, but she wasn't there. That same day, Kelvin and I were in the library laughing and talking when – out of nowhere – I got snatched up by the back of my shirt collar and dragged into the hallway. When I turned around, I was looking up into Rodent's face. He didn't say anything to me, but he just drew back his arm and slapped me across the face in front of the other students. You can't imagine how hurt, angered, and embarrassed I was! Kelvin was the only one who didn't laugh at me. Rodent told me to stop being a class clown as I stood there in shock, not believing what was happening. Then the librarian came out and explained to Rodent that I had done nothing wrong. She told him that we were allowed to laugh and play because the library was really our recess area since the school didn't want us going outside with all the gang violence. While she explained this to Rodent, I hated him more and more. Worst of all, he never apologized. He just gave the excuse that my punishment was for the times I had acted as a class clown and he hadn't caught me. His sad excuse didn't work – the damage in me was already done, and I was at an age to hold grudges.

I knew there would be more trouble at school with gangs, but I reasoned that I would have the upper hand over those kids when many of them transferred to George Henry Corliss High School, a Vice Lord gang school. I would no longer be outnumbered or bullied. I would one day have my revenge on those who chased me home from school every day from the Gangster Disciples and Black Disciples gangs. At Corliss High School, my gang would outnumber theirs. Yet, grammar school was another matter – it was torment. Nobody cared that my grades were all F's. I "graduated," but they didn't let me go to the eighth grade field trip, nor to the luncheon, nor to graduation! No one reached out to me – no one, that is, except Mrs. Thompson. She tried to help me, but, by that time, she needed a whole support team because I had stopped caring.

I was so tired of getting beaten up at school and so tired of getting beaten up with the extension cord at home. How could life be like this every day? I know at school they knew something was wrong at my home, but no one ever said anything to try to help us. The teachers saw bruises on Jarmal and me, but never once did they ask us anything or report it to the office – not even when it was hard for me to sit down at my desk! They just turned their heads the other way, not even acknowledging the pain that I was in. I didn't like pain.

It seemed that the more bad things happened to me at school, the worse my beatings at home got! Yet, through my sufferings, Demar, Kelvin, and Ahmad were always there for me. They knew how we had it at home, but they couldn't do anything about it. They were just kids too, so we all just tried to cope with the life we had. These are a few of my experiences during my years at Alfred D. Kohn Elementary School. Now let me finish telling you about "home sweet home"!

Home Sweet Home

Home Sweet Home! is a place to lay back and relax,
    but Home Sweet Home! is where I always felt attacked.

Home Sweet Home! is where I should feel safe.
    but Home Sweet Home! was not a happy place.

Home Sweet Home! should be happy and carefree.
    but Home Sweet Home! "Hide your tears so the neighbors can't see."

Home Sweet Home! a place to grow up and have fun,
    but Home Sweet Home! was more pain than warming sun.

Home Sweet Home! a place for childish play.
    Home Sweet Home! was why I'd run away.

Home Sweet Home! is where the heart is to be content.
    Home Sweet Home! Is where I felt abandonment.

Home Sweet Home! was where I felt scared the most.
    Home Sweet Home! is where evil was seen up close.

Home Sweet Home! is how it was supposed to be.
    Home Sweet Home! never felt much like a home to me.

Chapter 6
Home Sweet Home

"Time is like a snowflake – it melts away while we try to decide what to do with it."

– Anonymous

I have done my best to think of happy times at the house on South Prairie Street, but the good memories are overshadowed by the bad. Don't get me wrong – there were good days and pleasant family times! For example, once a year we went to Six Flags America amusement park, and sometimes we would go fishing. Of course, the reason we went fishing was that Rodent wanted to go fishing. From what I could see, family decisions were what Rodent wanted. Kids weren't considered. Many times I thought they believed their lives would have been better without us. What I resented the most was that Rodent didn't work. He had no job or anything special to do all day. He just collected his Social Security check every month, while my mother worked very hard to provide for the family, and all her money went into Rodent's pocket. She bought him a new car and covered the car payments. While he drove a brand new silver '94 Chevy Caprice, she drove an '84 Chevy Cavalier. For a while, she didn't have a car, and he would take her to and from work. She gave up everything for him – many friends and, finally, even her kids.

The period from 1988 to 1993 was crazy. I don't remember events in the order in which they occurred, but I do remember most vividly all the beatings I received with an extension cord. One time we were being punished for something like not taking out the garbage. Jarmal loved cartoons, so when Rodent would take mom to work, Jarmal would turn on the TV and watch cartoons – a surefire reason for punishment. When Jarmal heard Rodent returning from dropping Mom off, he would quickly turn the television off. Rodent would feel the back of the TV and see how warm it was. Then we would both get the extension cord before leaving for school. It didn't matter that I had been in the kitchen not watching television, I would get a beating just like Jarmal, for Rodent simply assumed that I had been watching it too. It didn't matter that Jarmal told him that I wasn't watching television, he would still beat me for it. On the other hand, when I did something wrong, only I would be beaten.

Many times after church on Sunday, we would go over to Great-Grandma Theola's house so that my mother and Rodent could have some time to themselves. I used to love it because I knew there was always plenty of food there ready to eat. Grandma Thea would meet us at the door and direct us to the food in the kitchen. On one Sunday she told us there was hot-water corn bread, fried blue-gill fish, and pound cake for the taking. I remember being pretty hungry, so I went right into the kitchen, where I was met by Great-Grandpa Nate. He pointed to the fish in the microwave. When I opened the door and looked in, I lost my appetite. Grandma Thea had fried the fish with its head still attached! When Mom came in, she saw me eating the corn bread by itself and asked why I wasn't eating any fish. Then she saw it, as I had, and ripped its head off. Yet, I still couldn't muster up an appetite to eat it. The sight of the fried fish head was just too much for my young mind and stomach to handle.

Somewhere in the early 1990s, my mother and Rodent got married at the family church on the west side of Chicago. Jarmal and I were ushers, and we handed out the programs for the service. When Rodent and my mother were up front saying their wedding vows, Rodent had a hard time trying to talk with his false teeth in his mouth. So, right in the middle of his vows – in front of the whole church – he took his teeth out of his mouth. I thought that was the funniest thing I had seen in a long time, and I must have laughed aloud and giggled to myself for twenty minutes or so! When the service was over and it was time to eat, all the kids went downstairs and sat at a table. We all picked up a butter knife and fork and started banging on the table, yelling, "We want to eat! We want to eat!" When it was time to eat, a lady took me aside and said that I could not eat until later. I didn't understand. "That was *my* mom who just got married," I said. But the lady didn't care. Now I was mad, hungry, and upset, and I began to cry. I was about to run out of the room when my mother grabbed me and asked what was wrong. After I explained to her what had happened, she went and said something to the lady. Then she came back and hugged me and took me to get something to eat. For the second time in my life, my mother looked out for me! Later on, I got to see the wedding on video, and I did look sort of funny laughing like that.

Sometime later – I believe it was after the wedding – Jarmal and I came home from Kohn Elementary School, and Rodent met us outside and made us sit on the front porch. After a while, he came outside and told us that our mother was upset because our aunt had been murdered. Yet, on a kid's level, something worse also happened that day. We went

Chapter 6 *Home Sweet Home*

over to Great-Grandmother Theola's house when we first heard that my cousin Stacey had just won a trophy in cheerleading. She was so happy coming home to tell her mother about it, and then she was greeted with the news that her mother had just been murdered! Listening to and seeing all the screaming and hollering was just so horrible, and all this time Jarmal and I were on the front porch at Great-Grandma Thea's house. Poor Stacey! We had to stay there a couple of hours, and then we finally drove home, which sure was a long, quiet, sad drive. Never once did anyone ask Jarmal or me how we were feeling about it all.

It wasn't until the next day that I found out from a newspaper at school how the murder had occurred. When I talked to my cousin Packey on the phone, he told me she had been found naked in a forest, stabbed with the sharp end of a crowbar. I remember hearing that another body of another woman had also been found. The news reports said my aunt was a prostitute, but she never was, so my Grandmother Edna called the news channel to complain. All that didn't matter to me. It doesn't take a genius to see that for two women both to be murdered and found naked in a forest preserve meant that there had been foul play. That was the last I heard of it. I don't even know if they ever caught the murderer, but I really would like my aunt's murder to be solved.

A while later our Great-Grandfather Nate died of cancer. I can recall seeing him in a hospital bed in the dining room of their house, and Grandma Edna was taking care of him. He had huge, black blisters all over his body. After he died, I don't remember crying at his funeral. Neither do I remember crying at my aunt's funeral. I never really knew them. It's sad when one's own family are strangers. We just knew that we were related. I didn't really know my Grandmother Edna, but she had our respect because she was our grandmother. I regret never having the chance to know her better because she was a drug addict and an alcoholic. I remember once catching her sniffing powder cocaine. I was shocked and lost respect for her over it. I wish there had been a way to make it better, but I lost her before I could. Jarmal and I were left to deal with our feelings over the death of our grandpa and aunt on our own. Affection was only between Mom and Rodent.

I don't know at what point it started happening, but Jarmal used to eat a lot. Of course, any parent would know that growing kids need to eat. Yet, in our house, when we would ask for something to eat, our parents always told us "NO!" It happened without fail. All the food we had was always theirs. So Jarmal used to look for things to eat. The only things we could freely eat were ramen noodles and Kaboom cereal. Yet, Rodent could eat whatever he liked; he had all the chips, ice cream, cakes, and fruit he wanted. We were never good enough for those items. If we got anything special, it had to be Rodent's leftovers or maybe a handful of chips. It was never anything of our own. Sometimes Jarmal would sneak into the cupboard and get my mother's slim-fast candy bars. Mom noticed, and she wanted to find out which one of us was taking them. So, one day she exchanged chocolate ex-lax for her candy, and the next day Jarmal was "wedded" to the bathroom.

To this day I hate caramel cake, Kaboom cereal, and Almond Joy candy bars. Why? It is because Rodent used to eat caramel cake and coffee almost every morning, and we could never get any. Yet, one day Jarmal must have taken a very small piece of it, and Rodent knew because he had it marked. He beat us unmercifully. All that for a tiny piece of cake? It proved to me that sharing was not caring! Why would a person do that? What was that supposed to teach us? All it did was make me hate Rodent and caramel cake!

Why did I hate Almond Joy candy bars? We used to go to church on Sundays, and on the way to church, Rodent would smoke marijuana and get the munchies, so he would stop at the gas station to get an Almond Joy. We hoped that he would get us a bag of chips or something, but nothing ever came our way. He would get himself an Almond Joy and get my mother a bag of hot Jay's potato chips, and that was it. However, Rodent had no teeth, so, when he had eaten the Almond Joy, he would spit the almonds in his hand and a couple of times he gave them to Jarmal. When my mother saw it, she slapped the nuts out of Rodent's hand and said, "That's nasty!" I was in the back seat with a disgusting look, shaking my head, and angry at Rodent.

I don't know when this happened, but one day we came home from school and found padlocks on the cabinets, pantry, and refrigerator. Why would people stop children from eating? It didn't make any sense to me. I guess they were trying to lower the household budget by denying their children food! Yet, it only caused more heartache and anger. Deep inside, I hated those locks.

With all the abuse going on every day in that house, my life was in turmoil. I remember our toy poodle "Butt-Butt," who wasn't house broken. My parents used to rub her nose in her waste and beat her with a newspaper. I remember her relieving herself on the new carpet and getting hit with the extension cord. Whenever this would happen, she would hide under the tub for days and would only come out in the middle of the night to jump into my bed when everyone was asleep. I would rub her little back and could feel the welts on her skin swelling up, and I'd tell her that it was OK, that they didn't know any better, but, of course, she didn't understand. As soon as the sun came up, she was back hiding under the tub. Poor Butt-Butt!

One day I was attacked at school and got suspended, so I knew I'd be getting another beating when I got home, but, this time, it turned into torture. I was tired of getting hit with the extension cord, so I grabbed it and took it. Suddenly, there was pandemonium! Rodent and my mother jumped on me, tied me down spread eagle to the four posts of the bed, and took turns beating me. There's nothing worse than getting a tag-team beating! I was bleeding from my thighs to my lower back. After a while, they let me go and told me to clean the basement. I went down there, and, by this time, we

Chapter 6 *Home Sweet Home*

had another dog, a pit bull named "Miss Thang." As I sat on the couch holding her in my arms, I decided I would run away. (I will describe my run-away days in the next chapter.)

When I was in that house, I could not understand the abuse that we received at the hands of both Rodent and my mother, but mostly Rodent. I remember one time that I made my mother mad by snatching the extension cord from her. She slapped my face and then punched me in the stomach, causing me to drop to my knees – I couldn't breathe! In the end, she felt guilty for what she had done. Their discipline was always way overboard, but in their minds, they thought they were doing the right thing!

There was nothing wrong with the chores that we had to do around the house, but I became the sole cook. I learned how to cook by watching my mother cook, and she was, hands down, a great cook and teacher. Every night I ended up cooking dinner for the family, and every morning I had to cook Rodent two pieces of pan-fried toast, four pieces of bacon, and two sunny-side-up eggs to go with his coffee. He loved strawberry jam on his toast, while breakfasts for Jarmal and me were cheap government Kaboom cereal or Mini-Wheats and powdered milk. The beatings went on for years. These are the only memories I have of that house.

One day, after coming home from school, Jarmal and I were hungry, so I went in to cook two packages of ramen noodles. I heard a crunching noise. I went to the back porch and there sat Jarmal eating dog treats! The treats were like bacon strips for dogs, even looking like bacon, though certainly not smelling like bacon, and so I said to him, "Dude, what in the world are you doing? Just cook yourself a bag of noodles."

He answered me, "I hate noodles. That's all we ever eat."

I said, "Seriously," and then left him with his doggie treats. Moments later, my brother came in and tried to justify his eating of the treats, saying, "They aren't that bad – try one." I refused. Later he was eating raw potatoes with salt and hot sauce. I guess he really did hate ramen noodles. I, on the other hand, embraced ramen noodles; they were my friends. They were always there when nothing else was. I couldn't blame ramen noodles that my parents were like they were; ramen noodles saved my life, and to this day I still eat them.

We did have some good holidays, but only because other people were around. I remember New Year's Eve one year when the adults got drunk and my mother left to drop off her friend Sonya Rivers. Rodent didn't want her to leave because he was jealous and thought that my mother was going to be with some guy since Sonya was so good looking. They got into a fist fight and tore the house up. My mother ended up leaving with her friend, and Rodent chased them out and shot out the back windows of the car. One of the bullets lodged in the headboard inches away from my mother, but she forgave him. Many times when they would get into an argument or a fight, my mother would go to "Toys R Us" and buy five to seven video games and we would get to play them with her. I hated to see our parents fight, but we put up with it to be able to spend time with our mother.

The first time I smoked marijuana and drank or smoked a cigarette was in the presence of my mother in our own house. She said that she would rather that we do these things around her than to get something bad out in the street and die. She thought we were smoking and doing drugs. She didn't know that, at the time, we were totally free of such things.

I remember Rodent entering our room at 2:00 or 3:00 a.m. to wake us up to whip us with his extension cord because we forgot to wash a couple of dishes or because we didn't take out the trash. To this day, I wake up between 2:00 and 3:00 a.m. in the morning – I am a very light sleeper. The things we were beaten for didn't make sense to me.

Run, Baby, Run

Run, Baby, Run! Get as far away as you can.
    Run toward the sound of the police siren.

Run, Baby, Run! Get away from all the pain.
    Hide all your tears in the rain.

Run, Baby, Run! In that house there is no love,
    But God is watching over and He sends His love from above.

Run, Baby, Run! There is no abuse from them anymore.
    It won't happen again like it did before.

Run, Baby, Run! There's no need for you to fear.
    Though you found a way to escape from them,
    there's no time for you to cheer.

Run, Baby, Run! You can relax now and get some sleep,
    With your tears all dried and fears piled up in one big massive heap.

Run, Baby, Run! Run, Run, Run! Ru-u-u-u-u-u-u-u-u-n-n-n!

How can this be?

You had to run to the horrible streets just to be free!

Chapter 7
Run, Baby, Run

You will always gravitate toward that
which you secretly most love.

– James Allen

Before I write about my runaway days, I want to make something clear to any young person who is reading this: Please don't ever think that the answer to your problems is to run away. The world is a very cold place, and I don't recommend finding your comfort there. If you are in an abusive situation of any kind and need help, go to someone you trust, like your teacher, your neighbor, a policeman, a fireman, a doctor or a nurse, a librarian – just tell somebody you need help. You don't have to face it alone. The street is not the answer because, although there are no rules out there and it may seem like fun, it's not worth risking your life. And for you parents: *never* put your kid out on the street. The outside world will use and abuse them. If you don't want kids, stop having them, and, for the ones you already have, take them someplace safe; give them a chance to live; give them a life. Don't take it from them. Remember, any of you who are abused at home, never run away, for there are *real* monsters in the streets.

When I ran away, I didn't care about a lot of things, so I ran to where I thought people cared about me, which was my gang. In the span of about a year and a half, I ran away from home about seven times. The first time I ran away, I was gone for three days. I slept in an abandoned car in a garage. My brother would throw me a change of clothes from his window, then I would go to my friend Kelvin's house and take a shower. The only people who knew were the neighbors because they noticed I was outside the house after the streetlight came on. I finally went back home out of hunger. When I came in, I would have liked to have heard: "I'm glad you came home. I missed you." Instead, I got, "The little idiot don't even know how to run away right. He came back because he was hungry." That's what Rodent said after laughing. He thought it was funny, but I surely didn't.

The second time I ran away was after another beating. I waited until Rodent was gone, then I left. This time I was gone for two weeks, and this time I took a couple of cans of corn, a box of Chex cereal, bologna, bread, and noodles. However, I forgot to bring a can opener, so the can of corn didn't do me any good. I ate the bologna in one day, and all that I had left were a couple packages of noodles. "Still," I vowed, "I will show him. I won't come back home because I'm hungry. No, sir!" Yet, I knew I couldn't stay out much longer – I had to return! I hadn't figured it all out yet, but I knew I would get it in time.

Another time I left was after getting suspended from school. I didn't even wait until Rodent or my mother got home. I just bagged up some clothes and left. It didn't make any sense to stay and explain myself. I knew I'd get a beating, then likely I'd get fed up and run away anyway, so why not just run away first without getting a beating? And that's just what I did, but I didn't run far. I ran only a couple of houses down.

It was about three weeks before Christmas, and Rodent and my mother didn't even have the presents out. I went to my buddy Kelvin Thomas's house and told him what had happened. He didn't want to get in trouble, so during the day I would stay out in the streets, and at night I would go to Kelvin's house. I would put a chair up to his window and climb through the window at about 10:30 or 11:00 p.m. and jump in the bed with him. He would pull the bed out and away from the wall. He would lay headed one way, and I would lay headed the other way. He would always keep some of his dinner for me so I could eat at night and in the morning too. Then, in the morning, I went back to the streets until night.

About two days before Christmas, my brother told Rodent where I was. I was laying in Kelvin's bed when I heard his mother coming. I rolled out of the bed right to the floor, Kelvin pushed the bed back, and I hid under the bed. Kelvin's mom found me and told me what was going on. Then she explained that I had to leave because Rodent and my mother threatened to call the police and press charges against her for harboring a runaway minor. I walked back home and didn't speak to anyone; I just stayed out of their way.

When Christmas came, it was sad, but I was so used to being hurt that I just pretended that I didn't care. Jarmal had more than plenty of presents, and I just sat there with a blank look, watching him open them all up. I could see the disappointment in Jarmal's eyes – he didn't like this at all, and he looked very uncomfortable. Then, when they got down to the last present, they handed it to me, and I opened it. It was a pair of fire engine-red overalls, and they were too short. I hated those pants! They must have been trying to get me beat up, giving me pants like that to wear! Jarmal got good clothes. I just got clothes that nobody wanted. Rodent would buy $300 to $800 shoes

Chapter 7 Run, Baby, Run

for himself. In making Rodent happy, my mother neglected herself. She wouldn't even buy herself anything nice. And, of course, Rodent bought Jarmal name brand shoes like black suede Adidas. Then he would walk me over to Payless and get me cheap old XJ900s. Do you know how much fun I was made of every day? Kids were always talking about my cheap shoes! I had a terrible time dealing with it every day at school. It was just horrible! And even though I was bullied at school, my parents didn't care a bit. They would just discipline me again and pour more fuel on the fire within me.

Then one day I just couldn't take it anymore. I was so tired of people talking about me and so tired of the beatings that something had to give. Irritated with another kid in school, I angrily thought, *I am going to really pound this guy, and if Rodent touches me, I'm going to kill him in his sleep.* In my anger I repeatedly punched the kid's face, pulled a whole shelf of books down on him, and left him there. I walked out of school and thought, *Now it's time to get Rodent!* But, the truth was that I didn't have the heart to kill him. I am not a killer. I had always accepted my beatings, but the one I got after this episode was horrible. Rodent whipped me everywhere from my calves to my arms, and I ran away, even though it was cold outside. I ran like the wind, and all I had on was a pair of black shorts, white socks, no shoes, and a T-shirt. I knew I couldn't run to Kelvin's house because his mother had already said she couldn't help me, so I went to another friend's house. At the time, I was only about twelve years old.

The friend's name was Pelza. He looked just like Jarmal. I stayed in his basement with him, eating doughnuts and playing video games. It was cold outside and all I had on for three days were jogging shorts and a T-shirt. Finally Pelza asked me, "What's wrong, Brian? Why do you make those noises in your sleep? How come you have blood spots on the back of your T-shirt?"

I said, "Do you really want to know?"

He said, "Yes," and he promised that he wouldn't tell anybody.

However, when I pulled my shirt off and pulled my jogging shorts down, he panicked and ran straight to his grandmother. That beautiful, delicate little lady asked me to come up to her room and sit on her bed. Then she held my hand and asked me quietly what was going on. I knew that someone finally cared. I tried to avoid answering, but finally I decided that I would tell her. Before I could start, I broke down in tears and just cried and cried. She laid my head down in her lap and rubbed the back of my head, and she said, "Just get it out, get it all out."

I just couldn't stop crying. After what seemed like four hours, I got up, took off my shirt and pulled down my jogging pants. When she saw the whippings, she gasped and said, "Oh, Lord! Help us, Jesus!" Her reaction told me how bad they were.

She gave me a warm bath and rubbed cream all over my back and legs, and, after about a week of healing, she called me into her room and told me that Rodent had to be stopped, and she called the police. The police came and took me to the police station, and I filed a complaint. They took documents and photos, and they arrested Rodent and brought him to the police station. After an hour, I was back in a car with Rodent and my mother. During the long quiet ride home, I figured out what had happened. As a Freemason, Rodent had appealed for help to his fellow masons who worked in the police station. I realized then that I was on my own and would receive no help from the police. I went back home and went to my room. For the next week, Rodent didn't say anything to me, but just gave me angry looks every time I crossed his path. As far as I was concerned, it would have been just fine for him not to speak to me ever again, but, of course, that wasn't going to happen.

About three weeks later, my parents were back to their usual treatment of us, but this time, after another beating, I received a massive verbal assault from my mother. She said, "You insist on being bad, then you tried to get my husband locked up. I can't get another man. Do you think that I am going to choose you over him? If I have to make a choice, I would choose him. I am not about to lose my man. I choose him."

Then, somehow, the conversation switched, and we were talking about Jarmal. She said something about how Jarmal was going to have it so much easier in life because he was light skinned, and that white people weren't going to treat me the same because I was dark skinned. The thought blindsided me, but I realized then that I would never look at her the same again. Now I understood why Jarmal was treated better and got the best clothes. I always knew they had treated him with favoritism, and now my mother had stated it outright. That night when they went to sleep I thought about bashing their heads in while they slept because they obviously didn't care a thing about me. Yet, I still had a heart, and I wasn't a killer, so I did nothing. Instead, I took $5.00 out of Rodent's wallet and rode the train to Aunt Bonnie's house in the projects.

Life with Aunt Bonnie was very different than life at home. There were house rules and chores, but they weren't stifling like the rules at my house. Neither were there beatings. I was free and safe. I could eat when I wanted and go outside when I wanted. The only thing was that I had to be back in the house by 9:30. I got to spend time with my cousins Cedrica, Packey, Val, and my aunt, my substitute "Mom." However, the fun was short-lived.

After about two weeks I went back home, and the cycle repeated itself. This time I rode the train all the way to the west side of Chicago and stayed with my Aunt Earlene for about a month. Living with her was a lot like living with Aunt Bonnie, but this time I hung out with my cousins Joe, Nathan, Justin, and Lacey. Though I have not written much about my two wonderful aunts, I do appreciate them both. They tried to protect Jarmal and I, but my mother yelled at them to stay out of her business.

Once when I ran away from home, I rode the train and slept on it for days, spending the day outside and sleeping on the rooftop. One time our gang chief saw me and put me up in a hotel. It was only by the grace of God that I was safe during all of the times I ran away. Ten percent of the kids who run away from home never make it back.

My Little Angel

My little angel was the cutest thing I had ever seen, and she had a heart of gold.
    My little angel was not able to tell me how my life would unfold.

My little angel couldn't show me that I was heading down a hill of self-destruction.
    I should have listened to my heart and gotten my
    life together by getting my education.

My little angel, with her beautiful eyes,
    helped me see things I needed to recognize.

My little angel helped me deal with my anger.
    She couldn't know how often she kept me from danger.

My little angel helped me stay content.
    It was through her I wanted to change my life and repent.

My little angel has grown up and is gone, and my life hasn't been the same.
    My missing you and worrying about you brings me much pain.

I believe that you were chosen by the great God above,
    That's why you, Ireena, *my little angel*, are my precious little love.

Chapter 8
My Little Angel

"I am only one, but I am one. I can't do everything, but I can do something. The something I ought to do, I can do. And by the grace of God, I will."

– Edward Everett Hale

February 28, 1993, is a day I remember very well because it was the day I came home from school to find a beautiful baby girl laying on my mother's bed. They told Jarmal and me, "Hey! Come and meet your baby sister!"

It took me by surprise because my mother had not been pregnant. My parents explained that they had adopted her. I thought to myself, *In what universe should these two get to adopt a baby?* Jarmal wasn't happy about it at all, but when I looked down at her, she had a confused look on her face, and I instinctively reached out my hand to her. She grabbed my index finger and smiled at me. Surprisingly, in that very moment, I felt alive and important. Next she tried to eat my finger, and I discovered that babies try to stick everything into their mouth. They call this their "oral phase." When my parents told me that I had to move into Jarmal's room and give Ireena my room, I was more than happy to do so.

After a couple of days, Ireena's room was ready. Those first nights I saw the look between Rodent and my mother that said that they wanted to have a child together. But that was crazy – they were not fit to be parents! They drank, and Rodent smoked marijuana! I watched how my mother took care of my little sister, how she held her, how she changed her diaper, how she fixed her bottle, how she burped her after a feeding, and how she bathed her. I watched because I knew that, sooner or later, they would put her care off on Jarmal and me.

The first night she was in our home, she started crying in the middle of the night, and she was laying right between Rodent and my mother. I walked into the room, picked her up, went and fixed her a bottle, changed her diaper, and burped her. When she went back to sleep, I laid her again between Rodent and my mother. I did it again before I went to school. Then I rushed home from school to see her. That little girl was my heart. I promised her that I would keep her safe, and I became overly protective of her. There was nothing else that I really cared so much about, for I did not know Jesus at that time. My whole heart and my first priority were Ireena. Even when I ran away for beatings I would come back in a couple of days because of Ireena.

Every day I delighted in helping to raise her. I helped her learn to walk. I got up at night to meet her needs and stop her crying. I fed her when she was hungry. When she was weaned, I remember how she loved applesauce and pumpkin, but, oh, how she hated peas and carrots. She made the most disgusting face as she spit them out. Yet, I knew that she needed to eat them, so I would dip some mashed peas or carrots in the applesauce to fool her into eating them. She would stick out her tongue to taste the food, and if she didn't like it, she wouldn't open her mouth. When she touched her tongue to the applesauce, she opened her mouth wide and then was confused by the mixture of flavors that followed. However, my little trick worked. Then I would give her a spoonful of applesauce just by itself.

By then I was thirteen and taking on more and more of Ireena's care. Jarmal honestly didn't want anything to do with her and seemed jealous of the attention she received. Taking care of Ireena was the greatest thing that ever happened in my then miserable life! As a result of my taking on so many responsibilities with her, Rodent and my mother started giving me an allowance of a few dollars. Their reasoning seemed to be that they wanted to bait Jarmal into wanting to do something for her. Yet, he wouldn't have it. For me, taking care of my little Ireena was a delight.

By the time she turned a year old, we were putting her in a baby walker, and she walked non-stop! I had to watch her carefully because she would get into all kinds of trouble. One day I was coming out of the basement from feeding our pit bull, Miss Thang, when I saw Ireena coming out of the living room into the dining room with a disgusted look on her face. As I got closer, I could see why. She had a blackish ring around her mouth, and her hands were gray. She looked so pitiful, but I couldn't help but chuckle a bit. Poor little baby! She had gotten into an ash tray and eaten a mouthful of ashes! I carried her to the kitchen and rinsed her mouth out and cleaned her up. I asked her if she felt better now and gave her a popsicle, which I knew would make her smile.

When my parents set up Ireena's bed in my room, they put her bed close to the floor so she wouldn't hurt herself if she fell out. And she surely did not like staying in her bed! One night, at about 2:30 a.m., I woke up and found her trying to get in bed with me. I told her to get into bed with Jarmal because he had a bigger bed, a queen size, and I only had a single bed. However, he pushed her away, and I told her to come back to me.

Chapter 8 *My Little Angel*

Then, not only did she get in my bed, but our poodle Butt-Butt did too. She went right to sleep. The next morning, I awakened to find myself soaking wet from that little girl. It caught me by surprise, for I hadn't thought about that happening. Yet, I wasn't angry at her. I surely was glad that I still had the plastic on my mattress. Her crawling into my bet with Butt-Butt became a regular routine each night at about the same time. I believe she crawled in with me because she knew she was safe with me and that I loved her, and I certainly could live with that!

When she started babbling, she used to call me "Ba," which was short for "brother." She could babble on for an hour straight! She had so much to say, and not a word of it could I understand. Yet, she knew that she had my undivided attention. Nonetheless, after a while, a fellow wants a little peace and quiet. I didn't yell at her or push her away. I just went to the cabinet and got some peanut butter, and warmed it up a bit, and ate it on a spoon. Then she would take the notion that she wanted some too, and I would give her a spoonful of it. Since it was so thick, she couldn't talk, and it would give me ten minutes worth of quiet. She would cross her arms and look at me all mad. Then when she could talk again, she would want more peanut butter. The contradiction was puzzling to me, but I knew that, while she was eating peanut butter, she would be quiet.

One day Mom wanted to clean the house and asked my brother and me to take Ireena with us as we went to Evergreen Plaza to buy clothes or something. I jumped at the chance. We took the bus up to the shopping center on 95th Street and Western. By the time we got there, Ireena was crying and didn't want to be put down. I think she was just nervous around all the people. I didn't mind carrying her. Her warm little hugs around my neck told me that, if no one in this world loved me, she did, and I loved her too!

The mall was very exciting to her, and it seemed that whatever food she saw, she wanted. She saw chocolate cupcakes, and wanted one, so I got her one. She ate just a bite of it, and Jarmal had to finish it. She saw a soft pretzel – bigger than her face – and she wanted it, so I got it for her. She nibbled on it just a bit, and Jarmal finished it. She wanted food from Taco Bell and McDonald's, and, yes, she got it, and Jarmal finished it. I really spoiled Ireena that day, but I didn't care because I loved her so much. That day I ended up spending all my money on her and Jarmal, and we never bought what we went for. Jarmal even had to pay the bus fare for the ride home!

One thing I learned very quickly is that everybody wants to hold a baby, and it made me very angry that so many strangers wanted to hold Ireena! I didn't like sharing her like that. At church on Sunday, I had a hard time keeping up with her as she was passed from person to person. It made it hard paying attention to the pastor as I watched Ireena change hands like currency. Soon I would lose patience with it, and I would go get her and bring her back to my seat. Even in the hour without her, I missed her smile – I was her protector.

One day something really scary happened with her. Our parents were not at home, and two friends of ours, Ahmad and Demar, came over to visit. We were just sitting around talking when Ahmad pulled out of his waistband a .357 revolver and handed it to Jarmal. Ireena was in her room while the rest of us were in the dining room, and Jarmal sat down at the table and started playing with the gun like he was in a western movie. He cocked and re-cocked the gun and then spun it on his finger, and he was pretty fast. I went over and closed the door to Ireena's room where she would be safe while I went into the kitchen to fix her something to eat.

About ten minutes later, I heard her talking, so I went into the dining room to see what was happening. I saw Jarmal still playing with the gun, and Ireena was about three feet away from him, but directly in front of him. I didn't know if the gun was loaded or not, but to be safe, I went over to her and picked her up and yelled at Jarmal, "What in the world are you doing!" And as soon as I picked her up and turned around, the gun went off – *BLAM*! The bullet ripped right through the wall and would have gone right through Ireena if she would have been standing where she was just a few minutes before! My heart skipped a beat. Ireena started to cry, and I went to calm her down while Ahmad took the gun back. I walked over to Jarmal and exclaimed, "If you had shot my little sister, I would have killed you!" I said that because I was really angry, but I also didn't care about anything but her.

Later on that day the lady next door, Mrs. Donnie Jefferson, told my mother about the gunshot she heard, and Jarmal just told her it was Ahmad shooting in the backyard. My mother never told Rodent, and I never told on Jarmal, but I sure thanked God for being there at that moment to move Ireena out of the way of that bullet!

I was always there for my little sister. She didn't know that she was also there for me. With her at home, I was happy to come home from school. There were a couple of times that she ran to me when I came in. She would have a look on her face like she had been crying, and what would go through my mind was, "He better not have touched her!" I already knew that my mother wasn't going to say anything. Rodent did just what he wanted. And me? I was becoming more dangerous and didn't even know just how dangerous I was. I was way too protective of her because all I cared about was Ireena Washington! And I was about to find out just how dangerous I was.

Where Were You?

Where were you when I really, really needed you,
    When I was feeling down and blue?

Where were you when I had nothing in this cruel world to live for?
    That's when I really needed you even more.

Where were you when I was alone on the street and crying,
    When I felt I had lost my mind and thought of dying?

Where were you when I was bullied and made the outcast?
    I thought you were my brother and loved me all our past.

Where were you when I searched for you in my necessity?
    I guess you were in the neighborhood showing off your popularity.

Where were you when I needed to be brought from darkness into the light,
    When resolution to my pain came nowhere near my sight?

Where were you? Where were you?

Where were you when the clouds and sky became gray?
    What? I'm sorry! Is that the only thing you can say?

No! Where were you, Jarmal, when I most needed you?
    I'd been there to help you whatever you asked me to do.

Chapter 9
Where Were You?

"Every man has the same final destination: death at the end of life's road, but the path we travel makes all the difference. Some of us have maps and goals, others are just lost."

– Frank Herbert

By spring of 1993, I had become angrier than ever. The only good thing in my life was my little sister Ireena. I was glad that grammar school was over – no more running to avoid being bullied, no more being talked about, no more getting suspended for protecting myself. Nonetheless, I was still very angry. All I could think about was getting revenge. I was just so tired of all the hassle! I even "dropped my flag" twice to get out of the gang, but my brother talked me right back in for my protection. Gang life would continue to hound me.

My first gun was a .380 made of chrome with a pearl handle with a clip and a holster. I couldn't wait to try it out. After shooting out streetlights in the alley, I was hooked! At this time, my brother and I were fighting daily to keep the opposing gang off of us. The day that the Black Disciples shot at Jarmal scared him to death! That experience pushed my anger level off the charts, and I lost it! There was no more talking, we were at war! I ran up to 108th Street and Michigan and found the guys who shot at my brother, and before I could do anything, they ran. Since he was a good looking guy, Jarmal seemed always to be getting into conflict with people over girls. He was light skinned with long hair, and he had a job. Now I'd have to watch out for him.

On that particular day, he had gotten into trouble with someone again, and so we told him that, when he came home, he should avoid 108th Street and get off the bus at 107th Street and Michigan. Yet, he got off at 108th Street anyway and got beat up pretty badly. At the time, our gang was also at war with the Mickey Cobras street gang. We got a big surprise that day when one of them suddenly pulled up in their car yelling, "Your brother!" I was seconds from shooting that car to pieces because that is what I thought they had done to Jarmal! What a mess he was! His shoes were missing and he was all beat up and bloody. Rodent came out and took him to the hospital, and I called up Ahmad and asked him to bring me another gun. What he brought was a solid black glock .380. I took it and went up to 108th Street and started shooting. They shot back, but, by the grace of God, no one was hit. Yet, I let them know that I was a force to be reckoned with.

A couple of days later I returned to 108th Street, and there I saw two young men my age whom I knew to be part of the Black Disciples gang (the BDs) that had beaten up my brother. One had a pack of Newport cigarettes in his hand. I pulled out my .380, snatched the cigarettes, and shot seven times over their heads and ran away. For weeks the CVLs and the BDs were at war, and I didn't care a bit because I hated those guys. Half of them were in my grammar school class. One year they had all switched gangs from Gangster Disciples back to Black Disciples, but this didn't stop my anger toward them.

One day we were all having our meeting, and when we came out, we were jumped by the Four Corner Hustlers gang. Because of the attack, out of about twenty to start, only five stayed in the CVLs. Now what was going to happen? We found out that the Four Corner Hustlers and the Black Disciples had formed an alliance, a peace treaty, which made us at war with both the Four Corner Hustlers and the Black Disciples. Later on that night I was walking down the alley on 106 Prairie Street, right behind Kelvin's house, when a black '55 Chevy Impala with black tinted windows cut off the alley, and I stopped in my tracks! My adrenaline was pumping because I didn't have my gun. What happened next is like something in a movie, because just then it started to rain hard, and I took off running in the opposite direction. There was a steel garbage can at the end of the alley, and I dove into it head first. What followed was a hale of bullets! I must have heard at least thirty rounds ricochet off that garbage can! When it was over, I ran home. That night I thanked God for keeping me alive.

That whole summer we were at war, and I was afraid to take Ireena anywhere because she might get hurt. And while I was Jarmal's backup, Jarmal wasn't mine. All he cared about were the girls, who seemed to always get him in trouble. There were a couple of times that he was chased home for messing around with someone's girl. That is just how he was.

The beatings at home continued, but I kept living with my parents because I didn't want to leave Ireena. One day after another of Rodent's beatings, I decided I couldn't take it anymore. Rodent was dead in my mind, and I was about to take him out. I went into the alley and waited for him to come home and turn into the garage. I was ready to shoot his car up when – from out of nowhere – Jarmal popped up and just looked at me. At that moment, he must have known what I was about to do, and he begged me

Chapter 9   *Where Were You?*

not to do it. He talked to me for twenty minutes, telling me that I didn't want to go to prison for murder and that our mother would never forgive me. He recognized that life might be better without Rodent, but the truth was we would lose our mother as well. Even though I hated Rodent and was angry at my mother, I really wanted my mother's love, even though she was under Rodent's control. He controlled her life and ours. Yet, Jarmal talked me out of what I had in mind to do. I finally walked off. Rodent never knew how Jarmal saved his life. Yet, the irony is that Rodent gave Jarmal a terrible beating that same night for not taking out the garbage.

September came around, and it was time for school again, but learning was the furthest thing from my mind. I was still angry, and revenge was all that I could think about. I kept thinking about all those guys who chased me home and beat me up in grammar school all that past year! As the saying goes, "Revenge is a dish best served cold," and now I had the upper hand. In our first days at Corliss High school, I started a riot every day for about two weeks. I had all the Conservative Vice Lords beat up all the Black Disciples. They were going to feel my wrath through their pain! And they did, until they dropped out of school. They knew that, if I ever saw their face at Corliss High School, I was going to draw blood.

Everything in our house was the same. The beatings were the same, the chores were the same, the verbal abuse was the same. There was nothing new. Rodent came close to death so many times that he never knew about. I honestly believe that they thought that their brand of tough love was the best solution. Yet, it didn't work. The only time they acted decently was when we were in public together. There they hid their true selves.

Shortly after my fourteenth birthday, I came home from school and heard Rodent trying to get Ireena to stop crying by yelling at her. She was only about nine or ten months old at the time, and, just as I had anticipated, my mother wasn't doing anything to stop him. I don't even know why my mother was home, but I went in and asked what was going on. Rodent told me that Ireena was going to listen to him. I told him that she was just a baby and didn't understand, then I picked her up and she stopped crying. I told Rodent all he was doing was terrifying her, and he asked me to put Ireena down. When I did, he hit me, and we got into a fight. He was hitting me hard! My mother jumped in and tried to break it up, and I yelled at Rodent, "I hate you, you ain't my father!"

In that instant, I saw a look of anger and hurt on his face, and seeing how I had finally hurt him, I said it again. Before I knew it, I was laying across my brother's bed and Rodent was on top of me while my mother kept saying, "Rodent, let him go. Rodent, let him go!" I thought she was coming to my rescue, but that never happened. When Rodent got off of me, I looked at my mother with hope of some sort of comfort, but all she said was, "How dare you say that to him! He's been there for you since you were five," and then she told me to get out. I looked at her with surprise, but the thought that kept running through my head was, *I didn't choose him as a father; he was forced on me*. Right then I realized that I could not stay there any longer, and I left, never to live there again.

When I left, I went up to the house on 113th Street and Wentworth where all the CVL kids went when they ran away from home. I spent my time plotting how I would get back at Rodent. During that time, I was dating a girl named Kimkanglia, though we called her "Angel" for short. She was a runaway too. I left her alone one night at the house, and when I came back, she was laid out asleep with no underwear on. I leaned over and woke her up, telling her that she had to go home. It didn't take very great insight to figure out what had happened to her, and she was only thirteen years old. I had just turned fourteen and was crushed that somebody in the CVL would do this to her. At that moment, all my feelings of comraderie stopped for the Conservative Vice Lords.

About a week later, I was thinking about how to get some money and how to get back at Rodent. It was then that I decided to steal one of his guns. I went home and jumped the gate in the backyard. Then I climbed through the basement window and made my way across the basement and up onto the back porch. I then broke out the kitchen window. I went into his bedroom and found his stash. I stole his .38 special and about $20.00 in pocket change. I traded the .38 special for a glock .380. I had the new gun in my possession for only about six hours when Jarmal came out of nowhere, charging at me! Then he and I started wrestling as Rodent arrived and overpowered me, threw me in the car, and put the safety locks on as we drove home. All this time I had the glock .380 on me. When we got home, we started fighting again on the porch. I pulled out the gun and told him that I would kill him, but it was on safety, and we just fought some more until Rodent, Jarmal, and my mother finally tied me up and called the police.

At the police station, I was charged with unlawful use of a weapon, but I also pressed counter abuse charges against Rodent. After about three hours, I was put back in a car and driven home. When we got there, I found the window nailed shut, and I was locked in my room.

The next morning, they woke me up about 6:30 a.m. and told me to wash up. When I was done, my mother put me in the car, and we drove to the Cook County Hospital where I had to talk to some doctors, which ended in an altercation with them. They kept asking me why I was so angry and bad! I kept trying to plead my case regarding the abuse, but they only saw me as a lying child who wanted attention. Then, the doctors and my mother had a discussion. I don't know what they said, but the next thing I knew, I was on a stretcher in the back of an ambulance! Obviously, nobody believed me!

I arrived at Lake Shore Hospital a few hours later and had to stay in my room for about two weeks. I couldn't contact anyone. I remember that my nurse was a redhead with green eyes. The food was pretty good. Throughout my stay, which lasted about six months, the nurse had me keep a journal, writing daily everything I was feeling. The journal turned out

Chapter 9 *Where Were You?*

to be much like what I am writing in this book. The nurse told me that she had seen bad kids, and that I wasn't one of them. I could hardly believe it! Finally, after all these years, someone believed me and was on my side! It was amazing how easily I transformed when I was out of my everyday surroundings.

After ninety days, I had a meeting with my parents, which turned negative, and my nurse realized I didn't want to go back home. I stayed at the facility another three months and got angry and started a fight one day with another guy out of frustration. When the nurse arrived, I stopped fighting. However, the other guy went crazy, and we had to enter "time out." They sedated him and wanted to sedate me as well, but my nurse said that I didn't need it, and I didn't. For that little episode, I was put on room restriction for a week. Soon everything went back to normal. When my time was up, I was sent to Merryville Holding Place. I knew that I was in trouble when I entered. There were something like 900 boys there and 90 percent of them were Gangster Disciples, to whom I was a sworn gang enemy. My problems would only get worse if I stayed.

Later on that night, everyone who was on good behavior got to go to the Rainbow Skating Rink, and since I had just arrived, I was able to go. While we were there, a gang fight started, causing us to have to leave early.

I was glad it worked out that way because, when we got back and I took my shower, there was a man there interviewing us for a group home. Mr. Pitts was talking to all the young people, and I begged them to let me talk to him. When he did, I told him about my situation. I told him about how I was in one gang and the majority of the other guys were in another and how my life was in danger here. Then, after about three hours, Mr. Pitts spoke to all of us and told us that he could only take about ten boys to the new Alpha House Group Home. As he started calling off names, I figured that he would not call mine, but when he got down to the last two names, mine was one of them. I was so happy! I ran and got my belongings as I heard another one of the boys say that the group home was on 49th Street and Woods, and then he referred to "the guys over there." I knew what he meant. It was Gangster Disciples territory. My heart sunk because I hadn't thought that the group home would be in Chicago. My last words walking out of Merryville were, "This ain't going to be good," which meant that, since I was a Conservative Vice Lord, I was going to be a target again.

That was a long, quiet bus ride to the south side of Chicago. I was headed right back into the same horrible situation I had come from – I just couldn't escape the gangs.

A Lonely Child

A child of night, a child of day,
    Someone please rescue this child and show him the loving way.

Living in a foster home where no one loves this child, what is this?
    The lonely child was longing for just one hug or kiss.

When things went wrong, it was the child who had to bear the blame,
    Accepting beatings for another's wrongs is really such a shame!

All that the child ever wanted was a real mother or a father,
    But loving people didn't help, it was too much of a bother.

Now the lonely child is living in hatred and in fear,
    But deep inside he's praying for God to take him away from here.

It's sad that the child in this house who seems so bold,
    Feels so much pain that all that good in his heart grows cold.

For a child who never had a Christmas, nor celebrated his birthday,
    Your gaping mouth and stagnant tongue have nothing to say.

When will this child feel the warmth of love?
    Will it only be in heaven above?

Maybe it doesn't bother you that he never smiled.
    But what if you were that lonely child?

Chapter 10
A Lonely Child

"Human nature will not flourish, anymore than a potato if it be planted and replanted, for too long a series of generations in the same worn out soil."

– Nathaniel Hawthorne, *The Scarlet Letter*

When I got to Alpha Group Home, I was already angry. I didn't know how long it would be until opposing gangs caught up with me. I didn't tell anyone in the house that I was a CVL except a guy named "Red," who was also a CVL, and "Red" seemed to have a death wish. We were both in the wrong neighborhood to be identifying our gang affiliation. I did my best to persuade him not to jeopardize our safety, but he didn't catch on. He was a pretty big guy, so he thought he could just beat up everybody. What I tried to get across to him was that one person can't beat a mob! However, it did not seem to matter to him. Being in this group home wasn't the biggest problem, it was the neighborhood, and I knew my living there was not going to be safe. So, immediately after leaving Lakeshore Hospital where I had had a chance to change to a normal existence, I had to adapt back into survival mode!

Although I had some problems with the guys in the house, it was what went on outside the house that had me worried more. The house was in the heart of gangland on the south side of Chicago. Therefore, I could not go anywhere without taking someone with me. I had no form of protection to carry. I put on a façade that everything was fine, but inside I was really scared. I met the neighbor, a Latino lady who adored me. It seemed that her daughter had a crush on me as well. I hate that I cannot remember her name, but I do remember that she was a really nice person.

After a week of settling in, I was looking out my window one night about 11:30 p.m. when I saw a guy running out of a walkway between two houses, and then he ran down the street to a white Chevy, which he shot all up so that it crashed with about three or four people in it. I couldn't believe my eyes! I knew that I had to get my guns or not go outside. So either I stayed inside or only went to the front porch, the back porch, or the backyard. I surely did not wander around the neighborhood, even though there was a nice park next door called Cornell Park. I went there just once to play basketball.

While I was living in that home, the little Latino girl who had a crush on me was getting upset because another girl, who was named Brandy, kept paying attention to me. I knew that Brandy liked me. She was pretty and light-skinned, but she was in the GD gang. Knowing the danger, I really could not trust her. In fact, I could not trust anyone.

Every Friday we got our allowance and could decide whether we wanted to go to the Marklam Skating Ring or to the movies.

One time when we went up to the Marklam Skating Ring, nearly all my high school was there. I didn't know that so many people missed me, but it felt good knowing that I had some old friends and associates still there. That whole night I kept my gang buddies from bothering people at my group home, even though, at the time, I wouldn't have cared if they had beaten them up! Yet, I wanted no trouble that night, so I did what I could to keep things at peace.

A better neighborhood would have made the experience at Alpha House better for me and for others. The neighborhood had a negative effect on the potential for helping young people. Even though the supervisors in Alpha House could protect us from each other on the inside, they could not protect us from others on the outside. One time we were taken to a basketball game with another group home. The staff were only trying to do something nice for us, but they were very naive to the dangers around us. They failed to realize that there were limits to where they could safely take us. When we were done with our basketball game, the kids from the neighborhood would attack them. Our group home tried to help, but it didn't work. The kids from the neighborhood attacked the group home kids on the way to the van. The group home kids came home with cuts and bruises, though not with any life-threatening injuries.

For a while, things in the group home ran smoothly, until we asked for a dog. We ended up finding a little kitten, which we were able to enjoy for only two weeks. For some reason, "Red" took the little kitten outside, swung it around by the tail, as if he were working a one-armed jump rope, and then slammed the kitten down into the concrete! Everybody saw it and wondered why he did it. Some suspected that he was drunk. Whatever the cause was, suddenly everything turned chaotic. The guys jumped on "Red" and beat him up. I didn't step in to help him because I was so angry about what he had done to our kitten! The staff took the kitten to the vet. She was really messed up, yet she survived. After that, I really disliked Red and avoided talking to him. The group home eventually kicked him out for doing that.

Chapter 10 *A Lonely Child*

The home had staff who ran it. To protect certain people, I have changed their names. We'll call the person who worked there Napoleon, and we'll call his friend James. Napoleon could have been something like seventy years old. He introduced me to his friend James. One day when I was at Napoleon's condo, I thought something was weird. He had a SEGA video game hooked up to a fifty-inch TV. Was the old guy a video gamer? Not very likely. It made me feel very uncomfortable, so I asked to leave. Napoleon's friend James, who was thirty-four, seemed like a nice person, so we hung out together every so often. I was happy to find out that he lived only two blocks from my mother's house. Sometimes he would pick me up, and we would hang out all day with my brother and little sister. Then he would take me back to the group home.

When I attended Corliss High School, it was awful. I had to take the bus, traveling through numerous enemy territories. One Friday the line was drawn for me. We were planning to go skating that night, but on my way to school, I was attacked by some Gangster Disciples while I was still in the bus right in front of Harlem High School on 96th Street and Michigan. Then, after getting beat up, I had to go to school. On the way home, I was on the 47th Street bus and was attacked again by the Black Stones gang. I didn't tell anyone what gang I was in; so how did I get randomly beat up twice in a day? I know that a person can be randomly robbed, but randomly beat up? My life was painful enough that I didn't think it could get any worse. I stopped taking the bus home, and I would have James drop me off at 95th Street beside the Dan Ryan bus terminal, and a brother in my gang would pick me up and take me to school.

James and I started hanging out more and more, and he would take me over to 71st Street and Michigan to Chicago State University, where his buddies and family lived. When I didn't have any money, he would buy me something to eat. Often we would pick up some of his other friends – all were young people about my age – and take them to his apartment. We would smoke marijuana, drink, and party, and there was never anyone around to get us into trouble. (Neither was there anyone looking out for us.)

One night we went to Marklam Skating Ring, where I met Kristen Knox. She was a petite girl with pretty, long, black hair. She was very outgoing and fun to be with. I went over to talk to her, as she was hanging out with her friend Mi-Mi. I noticed that she had feet too big for her body. (Later I nicknamed her "Bozo" because of her feet.) Yet, that didn't stop me from getting her phone number! After we left and went back to the group home, I called her, and we talked for hours. I found out that she was in a gang called Blackstone, and she went to a school called Shepherd in Calumet Park. Our relationship was mostly friendship, though I had more feelings for her than she had for me. Perhaps it was that I needed someone to love me.

When my birthday came up, Rodent, my mother, and Jarmal came over and took me out to eat at "Old Country Buffet." We had a pleasant time and ate lots of food and talked. It felt like we were a family. If I had not hardened my heart against them, it would have been the perfect opportunity to connect as a family. However, I took the day as just another day. When we left, Rodent drove us back to the group home, and he and my mother gave me a little money. Jarmal gave me two dime bags of marijuana to smoke later with the guys in the group home to keep our emotions leveled out. Unfortunately, it tasted like wet dirt that had gone sour. As we arrived at the home, we said our goodbyes, and I gave my mother a hug. James had given me $50.00 and shoes for my birthday. Just as quickly as the day came, it also disappeared, and life went back to normal.

The group home was going well, but living there was getting very dangerous. By now, everyone knew I was a member of the Conservative Vice Lords. On Sunday I went to church with Mr. Pitts on 40th Street and Drexels. We sat in the balcony, and I spied Brandy in the choir looking beautiful as ever. After the service, I told her that eventually I was going to have to leave because, as she had seen, I was not safe.

Around November I left Alpha House and moved in with James. I was safe now, or at least I thought I was. I used to go to school and walk Jarmal home so nothing would happen to him. Staying at James's apartment, I could easily walk to my mother's house and see Ireena. James gave me money and took care of my needs. He seemed like such a nice guy. For once, everything seemed just too good to be true. That usually means that something is going to go wrong. It did, and it changed my life forever.

True Love

As I stand all alone under this midnight sky,
    I see dramatic clouds as they come floating by.

I gaze upon these clouds that have me feeling traumatized,
    In everything I see, I see the sparkle in your eyes.

I stare upon the stars to make a fleeting wish,
    About my true love whom I truly miss.

I pray that my wish might someday come true,
    Because I'm tired of standing in the night feeling deeply blue.

I still remember the first time I felt I was in love;
    I could hear the trumpet blowing, and music playing from above.

Whenever we were together, everything seemed so right,
    There was no fuss or argument, we never thought to fight.

I will do everything I can to keep my heart together,
    Because I don't want our shared memories to float off like a feather.

It's been some time since last I gazed into your pretty eyes,
    That to this day have me holding back my midnight blue cries.

Chapter 11
True Love

"What is this love that so many speak of with such apparent familiarity? Do they truly comprehend how unattainable it is? Are there not as many definitions of love as there are stars in the universe?"

– Frank Herbert

In this chapter I want to talk about the one I consider to be my first love. When I first went with the group home to Marklam Skating Rink, I was unsure of myself. I felt like an outsider. I knew how to skate, but I didn't want to get all sweaty the very first thing. So, after being there for an hour or so, I played a high-speed chase video game called "Chase H-Q," in which the player chases police then rams into their cars until they crash. (What does that teach an inner city kid?) I was playing the game and the siren overhead was going off, when, out of the corner of my eye, I saw a slanted-eyed girl in a pink shirt and blue jeans watching me play. I started showing off and spinning the wheel with one finger, showing my skill, alternating quickly between gas and brakes as if I were a NASCAR driver. When more and more people started watching, I got distracted and crashed my car.

The game was over, and the little girl stepped between the game and me and said that she wanted to play if I would put a quarter in the machine for her. The game cost 75 cents to play, which I think she knew, and I told her that. She simply said, "Can you put 75 cents in for me?" So, I did. Soon, however, she lost and wanted to play the game again. I put money in a second time. However, I couldn't do that many times more, because I only had a few dollars left. I didn't tell her that. I was a little surprised that she didn't ask my name, so I didn't ask hers either. However, her smell and appearance, her beautiful smile and her gorgeous laugh hooked me! Nothing else around me at that moment mattered, and my heart beat so hard that I thought she would hear it through my chest. My whole composure looked calm, but I wasn't calm at all. After what seemed like an eternity, she asked me my name and told me her name was Stephanie Peggs.

We exchanged phone numbers, and when I got back to the group home, I called her. We stayed up talking for hours. After a couple of days, I asked her to be my girlfriend, and she said "yes"! I almost hit the roof! We talked a while, and I told her a little about my situation. I was able to see her a couple more times when I knew I loved her. She was second only to Ireena, and I wished she knew more than the little I had told her.

My mother gave a convention for the "Masons and Eastern Star" at the Rainbow Skating Rink, and my mother and I and four others picked Stephanie up. That made seven of us in the car, with my mother driving. Stephanie had to sit on my lap. As we drove, I noticed that her head kept jerking forward. I thought that it meant that she was uncomfortable, so I asked her what was wrong. She told me that Demar kept slapping her on the back of the head. That made me a little angry. I told him to cut it out, and he stopped. When we got to the skating rink, I just wanted to get away from everyone else and spend time alone with her. We put on our skates and skated a little while, held hands, played video games, and even shared some candy. I know that people say that young love is just infatuation, but I didn't see it that way. You couldn't convince me that I didn't love her. However, it didn't seem that she had as much feeling for me as I had for her. Yet, I knew she cared about me, and that was more than most.

When the night was over and it was time to go home, my mother was so drunk that she couldn't drive, and Ahmad had to drive us home. After dropping Stephanie off at her house, we made it home and Demar started talking bad about Stephanie. I got upset with him, and we started fighting. Jarmal intervened. Later on, Demar and I were still friends.

July 3, 1994, was another unforgettable day. It was Ireena's first time at the lakefront at the fireworks display, and I wanted to be there to share the experience with her. My mother told me that I should spend the time with Stephanie, so I did. We sat under a tree away from everybody and watched the fireworks, and it couldn't have been more romantic. I was only fourteen years old, but we acted like we were much older! That beautiful experience stands out in my memory from the harsh reality of what my life was and would become.

We talked on the phone a lot, and I began to realize she wanted to know more about my life, which was something I didn't want to share. I didn't want her exposed to the life I had. When we talked, it was like a lovely fairy tale. Yet, all this time, I was becoming more angry and hateful in my life, something I didn't feel she would understand. There was so much I couldn't tell her and that I didn't want to burden her with. She was the world to me, yet I knew that I had to survive and that I had to hide her from so

Chapter 11 *True Love*

much of my life. I started backing slowly away from her.

I wish I could have told her everything about me. Yet, if I did, what could I have expected? That she would want to spend the rest of her life with me? That kind of true love is for story books. It rarely happens in reality. She would come down to my mother's house wearing her school uniform for the Academy of Our Lady. I had a totally different experience. I had to protect her from it. Stephanie was such a ray of sunshine in my skies of gray, but our relationship didn't last forever.

Who Cares

Who cares if I am enduring hundred degree weather without a fan?
    Who cares if I am trying to cope with the street life the best I can?

Who cares if I wonder what's happened to me and all the crimes that I commit?
    Who cares if I don't want to live this life and would rather not submit?

Who cares if I am a prisoner in my mind and need help to be released?
    Who cares if I am hurting inside for loved ones now deceased?

Who cares if I hate my life and need a change in the master I would serve?
    Who cares that I hate living at home and would rather live on the curb?

Who cares if I wonder what is needed to go out and get a job?
    Who cares if I have to continue with my personal *les Miserables*?

Who cares if I have many dreams and goals unable to be filled?
    Who cares if living on the streets might get me killed?

Something within wants to change so I can reveal my heart and give my share,
    but, like I said, WHO CARES?

Chapter 12
Who Cares?

"I'm nobody! Who are you?

Are you nobody too?

Then there's a pair of us!

Don't tell – they advertise, you know."

– Emily Dickinson

When I moved in with James, life seemed good. We laughed, spent time together, and had parties. He was like the big brother I never had. We would drive all over Chicago spending time with his friends while he was making drug deals. I never got into drugs, and I never sold them. I was just happy to be out of my house but to be able to see my sister and Jarmal every day since his house was just two blocks away from my parents' house. However, my life had drifted to the point that I had lost whatever connection with God I once had.

Around December 13, Rodent and my mother left town for a couple of days and left Jarmal at home alone. Early that day I went to school looking for Jarmal and Kelvin but found neither of them. We had organized a little crew of about ten young men and five young women who were associated with different gangs. We called it OCU, which stood for "Organized Crime Unit." It was a name we took from a 1930s Dick Tracy comic book. The crew was like a kind of brotherhood. When the other gangs didn't see any of our crew around, they would jump me. That day I walked home angry because no one was with me to help me when I had always helped everyone else, and it was still dangerous for me to walk home from school alone.

When I got to my parents' house, I saw Rodent's car and thought that he must be home. I turned to go to my friend J. R.'s house, and I found, to my surprise, that the whole crew was there. I told them how I had been attacked earlier and complained that they hadn't been there to help me. They had been too busy planning a three-day party at my mother's house with only $5.00 among them. Suddenly, Kelvin came up with a plan for stealing beer. About five of us would walk up to an A&P grocery store, and four of us would grab two forty-ounce bottles of beer and stand in line while the fifth guy would open the door and then all four of us with two-bottles each would run out the door with the beer. That is what we did, and we ended up with twenty-four stolen bottles of beer, which we took back to J. R.'s house. As we prepared for the party, I saw a girl looking at me. I asked her, "What's up?"

And she told me that she liked me, so I asked her name, and she said, "Stephanie."

I said, "Seriously?" as Jarmal and I smiled at each other.

"Seriously!" she said. Of course, she didn't understand our knowing looks. Jarmal knew about the other Stephanie, and I thought to myself that it wouldn't be hard to remember this other girl's name. I then asked her if she was coming to the party, and she said "Yeah," and I just smiled at her.

Later on that night, when we started the party, it was horrible, just horrible. I was the only guy dancing. All the other guys were playing a video game. Before anyone knew what I was doing, I reached over and unplugged the video game and said, "What are you all doing? We're having a party, and all you want to do is play video games!" They gave me hateful looks, and I just walked off because I heard a horn honking at the front of the house and went to see who it was. It was James, so I went out to see what he wanted. He said that he wanted to know if I was coming home. I told him that I was staying at the party for a couple of days, and he said with an odd emotional tone, "To be with your girlfriend!" I didn't understand what the tone meant, but I knew that the way he said it made me feel uncomfortable, as if, for some reason, he didn't like my having a girlfriend. I would find out shortly why that was. However, for the moment, I just shrugged it off, told him, "See you in a couple of days," and went back into the house.

The party inside was still dead when I returned, and everyone seemed to be drinking way too much. Someone told me to check on Leslie, who was in my brother's room. Leslie was a big girl, but very pretty. When I went in to check on her, I found her laid out on the wooden floor, making an angel pattern, and extremely drunk! I kicked her lightly with my foot and called her name, "Leslie, Leslie." She opened her eyes, looked at me, then sat up like a vampire coming out of a coffin. I looked at her in surprise as she tried to pull my pants down. But I had no interest in what this drunk girl had in mind. I tried to leave, but she grabbed my clothes again. I escaped from her grasp like Joseph did when he fled from Potiphar's wife. I ran out of the room, locked her in, and found myself standing like that before my brother, wondering what had

Chapter 12 *Who Cares?*

just happened. Jarmal shoke his head and laughed at me. I didn't find the situation funny. I sent him back into the room to get me some clothes.

After a while, Kelvin got the party going as he started dancing with a girl, and everybody else started dancing. I was dancing right next to Kelvin when his girlfriend got tired of dancing and walked away. Kelvin followed her, doing little hops, and with every hop he would look at her and say, "Where you going? Where you going? Where you going?" I had to stop dancing because I couldn't stop laughing. Then I went outside to make sure the rival gang wasn't anywhere around, and Jarmal and I went to the front porch to talk. Just then a girl walked up with her friend. It was Stephanie whom I had earlier met at J. R.'s. She had put on makeup, and I didn't recognize her. As the party went on, I stayed with her and ended up spending the night with her on the couch.

Early in the morning we woke up to the smell of something burning. We walked into the kitchen and found Leslie drinking a beer and trying to cook pancakes and sausages. This was not good. The pancakes were the size of a plate and burnt, and the sausages were the size of quarters and also burnt. However, people were eating the burnt pancakes with Alaga Syrup, which is as thick as molasses. Things were such a mess that, when Stephanie asked me to walk her home, I was more than happy to do so. As Kelvin and I walked her and her friend home, I discovered that she lived right across the street from Corliss High School.

When we entered her house, we met her Aunt Sharon, her brother André, and her sister Regina. She then announced, "This is my boyfriend, Brian." I gave Kelvin a look that said, *Whoa! When did I ask her to be my girlfriend?* Yet, I said nothing and just went along with it. We ate breakfast there and then went back to the party, staying together for the next two days.

The next night was supposed to be a pajama party. It seemed strange that I was the only guy who had pajamas. Yet, that was only because it was required at the group home. The rest of the guys were walking around with their legs and knees all ashy-looking, as if they had been busting concrete with their knees. I was glad that Jarmal and Kelvin had the good sense to take care of the problem with lotion. The party was OK that night. Later on, as they got hungry, they ate spaghetti with butter, salt, and pepper. My new girlfriend took Kelvin and I to a restaurant for cheeseburgers and fries. The next morning, as I was walking her home, I ended up telling her that I was a runaway, and she offered for me to come live with her. I put her off, saying that I would think about it, but I was happy for the offer.

Then I ran back to my parents' house to help Jarmal clean it up before Rodent and my mother got back. However, as soon as I got there, I saw Rodent and my mother about to go in. As I entered with them, I was surprised to see the whole house clean. We talked about their trip, and they asked where I had come from. I told them about my new girlfriend Stephanie and that I lived with her, which was not yet true. After Rodent hit the button on the answering machine and got its messages, he asked me why there were three messages from a lady asking about where her daughter was and the party she was supposed to be attending there. My heart dropped into my stomach because I knew then that Jarmal would be in big trouble. So, as they both looked at me, I lied and told them that I didn't know anything about a party. Then Jarmal came inside and Rodent exploded. I knew what time it was, and they told me I had to go, but I knew that Jarmal would get a beating for this. He did, and Rodent put him on restriction for six months.

The week of December 17 I was over at James's apartment watching TV, when James brought us chicken nuggets, French fries, and fruit punch Kool-Aid. After a while, I got drowsy and passed out. When I woke up, something felt strange, and I couldn't figure out why I was in my boxer shorts. It occurred to me that I must have been drugged and raped. Yet, who could I tell? Since I was a gang member, everyone would just look at me funny. When James woke up, he acted as if nothing had happened, and he asked me how I felt. *How do I feel?* I thought. *You have never asked me that before.* Suddenly I understood why this thirty-four-year-old man only spent time with young boys. He and his weird friend Napoleon had been grooming me for this from the start. I immediately left and moved in with Stephanie.

For a couple of days, I kept the incident to myself. Yet, I told Kelvin that there was something untrustworthy about James. He told me that he would look into it. It took a while before I saw Kelvin again. While living at Stephanie's house, I was attacked by the Four Corner Hustlers. I didn't want James to know that I knew what he had done, but I had to return to get some clothes. After we had talked a while, I thought that perhaps I had just imagined what had happened, but the pain in my lower regions argued that it had been real. I wondered, *Could I have eaten something that made me feel this way?* I stayed overnight against my better judgment, but didn't eat or drink anything that James prepared. Later on, I poured myself a cup of Kool-Aid, and the next thing I knew I was passing out. I woke up and found blood in my shorts. I thought to myself, *Aw man, he got me again!* When I confronted him, he denied having done anything, yet he seemed to be gloating that I wanted it to take place. I couldn't take it anymore, and I left for good!

I went to the house where the CVL kids run away to and didn't tell anyone what happened. I finally saw Kelvin. For a couple of days, he denied that anything had happened, but then he came clean and told me that he had awakened in the middle of the night one time and found James bending over him in an obscene way. I asked him if he had eaten anything at James's house. He told me that he hadn't, so I realized I wasn't mistaken about what James had done to me. He asked me if anything had happened to me, and I said that it hadn't, hoping that by staying away from James's house, I would forget what happened and no one would ever know.

Chapter 12 *Who Cares?*

On December 24 I left the runaway house, and I went back to live with Stephanie and her friend Sharon. Shortly after that Kelvin got locked up for murdering the corner store clerk when he didn't even go into that store. Where Stephanie and Sharon lived was another house for runaways, and it was a party house. I felt I needed protection by getting the guns Ahmad had been holding for me. After I got my chrome .380 back from him, I went over and shot at the Four Corner Hustlers for four days straight. They never figured out that it was me. I lived there almost seven months and did all kinds of crazy things! I was in shoot-outs; I watched people get shot and die; yet I survived and lived through it all. These are not things to brag about, but this was the nature of where I lived and what I knew. Looking back, I know that the guys I hurt were someone else's child.

Then in June of 1995 I moved in with Stephanie and her mother at 139 Carey in East Chicago, Indiana. It was the best time I had ever had. I was problem free and didn't have to worry about anything except for a bunch of neighborhood kids shooting Roman candles at us on the fourth of July. When we got into an argument with they kids, they called their homies. When they came around, they were threatening Stephanie's brother, André, and I was sitting in the backyard in a lawn chair laughing while they went and got some bats. I asked them, "What are you going to do with that?" I jumped up with my .380 in my hand, and their hostility suddenly disappeared.

Stephanie's mother actually never spent the night at home; she was always down the street at her boyfriend's house. His name was Mr. Mason, and he was eighty years old. Stephanie's mother used to get a lot of money from him. He drove a truck, like the one Red Foxx had in *Sanford and Son"* and was a cool, funny, hard-working man. I stayed with them for about two months.

Sometime during the summer when I visited my mother, I saw James out trying to keep things looking normal. He gave me two concert tickets to the Amp Theater on 47th and Halsted. James often bought tickets and gave them to young boys. He often would do things for kids that their parents would never do to get on their good side, and these tickets were not cheap! I took Stephanie's brother, André, because he was a Gangster Disciple, and I needed him with me to be able to blend in. The concert was live, and I saw Ice Cube, Notorious Big, Bone-Thug-Harmony, Outkast, Puff Daddy, and a few more. I had a great time. André and I were in the second row, seats 56 and 57.

James also gave me gifts to keep me quiet about what he had done to me. It was like a hush-present to keep kids from telling on him about what he had done or what was going on in his house. Yet, without the gifts, I would have kept quiet anyway because I was too embarrassed and afraid to say anything to anyone.

On August 14 I had a feeling that something was wrong with Ireena, so I told Linda and Stephanie that I needed to go back to Chicago. That whole day they begged me not to go, but to stay at least two more weeks. I did not listen.

Even Regina and another girl named Sky told me to stay. Yet, with my feeling that something was wrong with Ireena, no one could have stopped me from going back. That night I asked Mr. Mason if I could catch a ride with him the next day, and he said I could. The next morning, August 15, 1995, at 6:30 a.m., I was in Mr. Mason's old truck on my way back to Chicago. Things could have been so different if I had only known how my life would change forever in going back to Chicago!

Questions

Why was I put in this horrible predicament when it had nothing to do with me?
    Why is my life so boxed up and confined when all I want is to be free?

What did I do to deserve such a messed up life? No one should have one like this.
    Have you ever had to protect someone before?
    Only a child, I kept my promise.

Why does my heart hurt and feel so sad? It's such a small thing; I really can't tell.
    Why was I born into this world when my life is nothing but a hell?

Why did I return to Chicago when I could have listened and stayed away?
    Can I tell God I messed up? I was never taught how to pray.

So many questions that nobody but God has answers for.
    I'm so tired of this! I just can't take it anymore!

Chapter 13
Questions

"Murder first exists in the mind. He who gives hatred a place in his heart is setting his feet in the path of the murderer, and his offerings are abhorrent to God."

– Ellen G. White, *The Desire of Ages*

Around 8:00 a.m. on August 15, I made it back to my mother's house and noticed that I didn't see Rodent's car. I went inside the house, woke up Jarmal, and asked him if I could see Ireena, and then went into her room. When I saw her, I called her by her nickname, "Boobie," then I called her nickname again, and she opened her eyes and smiled. I got her up, gave her a bath, and fed her breakfast. Jarmal left around 10:00 a.m. and went down the street to a girl's house, so I brought Ireena out on the front porch and watched her as she played in the front yard. Everything seemed OK.

Around 10:30 a.m. I was hoping Jarmal would hurry and get back before Rodent returned, but he never did. *Where is everybody?* I was thinking. Out of the blue, James drove up with his cousin – or so-called cousin – in the car. Immediately, James jumped out of the car and pulled a 9-mm gun on me. I thought that he was going to shoot me, but he didn't, and with my hands raised, I walked to the gate and called out to Ireena to go into the house, which she did. Then James started asking me questions about my two friends – seventeen-year-old Tyrice Reyes and eighteen-year-old Deveron Martin – complaining that they had broken into his house and stolen some of his things. I told him that I didn't know where they were. He thought I was lying. I told him that I had just gotten back into town, but he didn't believe me and kept yelling and threatening me.

I noticed that he lowered the gun and lowered his voice, indicating that he must have seen somebody coming, and I thought to myself, *Please help me somebody!* I didn't have the answers that James was looking for when, suddenly, I felt a tugging on my leg, and I looked down to see Ireena. At this point James put the gun through the fence and pointed it at Ireena's head and threatened to come back to kill Ireena and me if I didn't get his stuff back. I grabbed Ireena, hid her behind me, and promised to get his stuff. He said that, if I didn't, he would come back. At this point I told myself that I was going to kill him because I couldn't let anybody threaten Ireena and get away with it. As quick as he came, he left just as quickly. An exchange that lasted only a couple of minutes seemed like an eternity. Looking back later, I realized that this was the fear I had had about something happening to Ireena. I was glad that I was there to protect her and that I had been the one to deal with the situation and not Jarmal.

Five minutes later people appeared from nowhere, and Jarmal was coming up the block too. Where was everybody when I needed them? I was so angry! I called Ahmad, and he came and picked me up. I told him to drive to 71st Street between Michigan and King Drive and we would find James. There he was, at an Amoco gas station. We followed James and his "cousin" all day, even getting gas together, and he didn't even know it because he didn't know Ahmad, and I was hiding in the car.

Around 11:00 p.m., Ahmad dropped me off at home. I knew that James would return home alone, so I stayed on the block my mother lived on. Ahmad came back about 11:30 p.m. and gave me the .38 revolver that James wanted. I had a good idea where to retrieve James's stolen belongings. When I confronted Tyrice and Deveron, they tried to act as if they hadn't taken anything from James, but I told them that I wanted all of James's items and that I would take it back to him. They gave me his $200.00 gold bullet belt and some clothes. We were all sitting on the porch of a Krystal's house when I saw James drive past. You cannot believe how badly I wanted to get back at James for what he had done to me and for his threats on Ireena's life. I asked Tyrice and Deveron to go with me, and we walked over to James's house together. They were standing on the left side of the door as I knocked.

When James opened the door, I had a white towel in my hand with the belt and gun wrapped up in it. Tyrice and Deveron didn't come in when I did. It was dark inside, yet I could see James. He was grinning and totally naked! I couldn't believe it! He was gloating about what he had done to me. Something inside me snapped, and I unwrapped the .38 and shot him in the forehead. I heard him let out a wheeze. I turned on the kitchen light, blood was everywhere, and the room smelled strongly of iron. Hearing the shot, Tyrice and Deveron knew what I had done, and they instantly ran away. I tried to leave, but his body blocked the door, and the door had a right-hand, inward swing into the house and only opened about three to eight inches. I jumped out of the first floor window and ran to Tyrice's house with the gun and belt still in my hand. I stayed at Tyrice's house until the sun came up.

Around 7:45 a.m. I saw Rodent and went to tell him, but he just looked

Chapter 13 *Questions*

at me and acted as if I didn't exist. Then he jumped into his car and left. I saw Jarmal and asked him to tell Rodent and my mother, but he never did. He wanted to confront Tyrice and Deveron, but that just made the situation worse. I went with Tyrice and Deveron to James's house to get my belongings out, they went back to finish robbing James. We climbed through the window, and I ran to the back and started bagging up my clothes and the other things that I had left. Tyrice and Deveron took James's things, including his car key, and we went back out on the street as if nothing had happened.

On August 17 Deveron went over to James's house and saw that the police had not been there yet, and he told me to go get James's car in front of his house. I told him that I didn't know how to drive, but he didn't care. Apparently, he didn't want to be seen taking the car, and I was his patsy. I got the car and drove it a couple blocks, crashing into parked cars along the way, then I ended up parking it in an alley where I met Tyrice, Deveron, and Everett, who was about eighteen. How Everett got involved, I do not know. Deveron jumped into the driver's seat, Tyrice got into the passenger seat, and they left. Everett came with me back to Krystal's house where I waited for Ahmad to arrive. When he did, I told him about the crime, and he asked me where the gun was. I showed him, and he took the gun and hid it with Everett. Then I sat on the porch for hours, waiting in vain for Deveron and Tyrice to come back.

Around August 18 Ahmad and I were sitting on Krystal's porch again when the police came running through a vacant lot right next to her house and crossed the street to Tyrice's house. Now I knew that they knew, and I got up and walked off the porch right past them, and Ahmad left in the opposite direction. I walked past my mother's house, and once I got past them, I started running, never realizing that a person cannot outrun a walkie-talkie. They caught me a couple blocks further down, took me to the police station, and questioned me without my parents or a lawyer. At that point they didn't have enough to charge me with murder, so they decided to send me to the Juvenile Detention Center at 1100 S. Hamilton – based on a neglect warrant for running away from the group home and for unlawful use of a weapon when I had threatened Rodent that time. I sat in the police station for hours. Then they took me downstairs and put me in a visiting room booth for three days, and finally took me to the Audy Home. I stayed in my room for three days and then was moved to wing 5A where I stayed for almost a month before I went to court.

In court I got the neglect warrant thrown out, and my mother somehow got custody of me with a one-year probation for the gun charge. However, when I walked out of the courtroom in the hallway, the Chicago police immediately arrested me for first-degree murder. They took me back to 111 and Ellis Police Station where they had boxes and files of evidence against me. They showed me many statements made against me, and I began to realize that I had gotten myself into a whole mess of trouble. What had happened to the little boy who hated seeing people hurt?

After trying to force a confession out of me, a female prosecutor came in and told me that she was going to give me a needle if I didn't tell her what she wanted to hear. I just gave her made up stories until they finally brought my mother in, and she told me to tell the truth because the police and prosecutor didn't believe me. The prosecutor showed me the five-page statements against me given by Deveron, Tyrice, Everett, and Ishmael. I didn't try to act like I was innocent. I just did not want to have to explain what James had done to me nor that I was protecting Ireena. Moreover, because I didn't explain, the police and prosecutor made me out to be a monster.

After about eight hours of interrogation, they read me my charges and sent me back to the Audy Home. I was portrayed as an evil monster. The truth is that I was by then a rage-filled young man who had taken justice into his own hands. I was wrong for my crime, yet I wasn't who they portrayed me to be. I did knuckle under the pressure of my peers in stealing James's car, and I did make up stories to cover what I had done. A lost soul without Jesus and with no other help, I let murder grow in my heart.

In the three years that I kept returning to court not once did anybody ever ask why James was naked when he opened the door to me that night – not the police, not the prosecutor, not the judge, and not my public defender. (But how would they know what he had done to me unless I told them?) They must have asked themselves why. If they had asked, I would have felt like a hundred pounds were lifted from my shoulders. They looked at his death as a crime to solve and didn't consider what went before.

While I Am Here Waiting!

While I am sitting here waiting and fighting for my life,
    my so-called friends have stabbed me in the back with a knife.

While I'm kept here, I tell myself it's really not that bad,
    Yet, I'm so tired of living – my life is very sad.

Being in here is the best thing that could have happened to me,
    No more beatings or abuse, from them I am finally free!

Chapter 14
While I Am Here Waiting!

"Everywhere I see bliss, from which I alone am irrevocably excluded."

– Mary Shelly

When I got to the Audy Home, the staff couldn't believe that I had committed murder, and I was left to myself my first couple of weeks back. Then, they told me to get my things because I was moving to general population. That is when I realized how very serious this was. They told me that I was moving to 4K and was charged as an adult, so that when I turned seventeen, I would be shipped off to Cook County by automatic transfer.

After I got up on 4K, I noticed how nice and quiet it was. I put my things in my room and went into the day room and was sitting there when one of my gang brothers, Shaun, came up in the day room, talked to me for a little while, and then left. I noticed a short kid at the end of the couch brushing his hair and noticed from his tattoo that he was a Mafia Vice Lord, making him a gang brother from a different branch. I was watching TV when about six other kids attacked him and started beating him up, pushing him all the way into a corner. I hurriedly ran over and picked up his hairbrush and slapped one kid in the face with it. Now I was in a gang fight, and I had just arrived! According to gang law, I was obligated to help him. But the kid I was helping ran away, leaving me to fight alone! Staff members came in to break up the fight. I was beaten up and mad! Shaun didn't help, the kid who had been attacked ran, and all the other Vice Lords just watched! Gang loyalty had gotten me into trouble.

Facility officials put me in confinement for two weeks, and the day they let me out, I punched a kid right in the face and went right back into confinement. This time I was in a cell right under the girls' wing of 5K, and I would talk to the girl above me all night. Her name was Aja Scott, and we talked just to help pass the time, although we were kind of flirting with each other. Something to do in a serious situation to take our minds off of how messed up our lives were. The next thing I knew, they came to tell me that they were moving me to 4E, and when I got down there, it was horrible. I saw Derreck Hardaway, my childhood nemesis. He had chased me home all through my grammar school days, and I had chased him out of Corliss High School. Here I did my best to stay out of trouble, and that's when I saw my best friend Kelvin. He told me that he knew some people with connections who could keep me out of trouble if I got moved down there. Soon they moved me down to 4G where Kelvin was, and I learned that Kelvin was the master of ceremonies for the talent shows every Sunday night. He introduced me to Mr. Michael Hedges. That was the best thing to happen to me during the time I was locked up in the Audy Home.

Mr. Hedges was an older white, salt-and-pepper-haired man, 6' 2" and about 220 pounds, who was very good with young people. Because he made time in the home much easier, a person would do everything he could to always respect Mr. Hedges. He was the father that all of us needed. Every day I attended class in that building. Every day I was called down to Ms. Adams' office because some girl wanted to talk to me. Every day Ms. Adams would call my mother for me at work. It was so good to talk to her the little that I could. Then, when school was over, we would go back up to 4G and have study period from 2:30 to 3:00 p.m., and Mr. Hedges would come up and get me, Kelvin, and Zebulun, and accompany us to the fifth floor to 53 and 5K to pick up about fifteen girls – Mandi Jones, Dana Karlofski, Carmen McDonnell, Carole Twitty, Tasha, Joni Allen, Jenny, Janelle Browne, and a few others. This little group became my friends, and we would get together and put on a show for the sections of the home that were allowed to come down and watch.

After a while, our little group started a choir, and we put together a show for the staff and others. That was the first time I met Mrs. Miriam Hedges. She was a sweet lady who later would play a very important part in my spiritual life. Our group sang a few songs – "Swing Low, Sweet Chariot," "Revelation," "Joy," and a few more. We did not realize how talented we were, but the audience clapped after every song, and sometimes they even stood up! Mr. Hedges gave us the thumbs up, he was so happy about it all. My singing voice sounded like I was singing under water, so I stood between Kelvin and Zebulun and tried to blend my voice in with theirs. It didn't matter if I wasn't as good as everyone else – I was still part of a choir.

During the six months that I was in the Audy Home, Kelvin and I had a lot of freedom to move about. The caseworker used to tell me that all I needed was an elevator key because I seemed to be everywhere. It was so good to be trusted and to know that I was in good hands!

Another great moment there was "Temporary Lockdown Six," a play that we performed all week for the kids at the Audy Home, for the staff, and, the last

Chapter 14 *While I Am Here Waiting!*

two days, for our families. I played a guy named "Tyrone." My role was to repeat the words of a guy whom my character idolized. It was hilarious when I'd repeat what he said. I am already goofy, and the way I played the role I had everybody laughing so hard that they were crying their eyes out.

The last day of the show I was hoping that my mother would show up so she could see how well I was doing and be proud of me. It was just ten minutes before the show was to start, and I was standing by the door, starting to get disappointed when – to my surprise – in walked Great-grandmother Theola! She didn't see me, and I said, "Hey, beautiful!" She turned around with the prettiest smile on her face, and I gave her a big hug. Then, as I was hugging her, I saw Grandmother Edna and my mother coming through the door. After hugging them all, I had to hurry back and get ready for the performance. Don't you know that that night I put on the funniest and best performance of the whole week! Every time I opened my mouth, the crowd laughed. It was so much fun! After the show, we got to talk with our families before they had to leave. That was the last time I got to hug Great-grandmother Theola and Grandmother Edna.

One of the best things about the Audy Home was that I never felt like I was locked up for murder. Anyone under eighteen had to make a request for a special visit, which I made to see my family. I was so excited when my mother brought up Jarmal and Ireena! This was the first time I had seen Ireena since the day we had been threatened in the front yard.

It had been about a year and a month before. Our visit was great. I got to play with Ireena during the visit, and we all talked and ate chips and candy. However, as we were walking down a long hallway at the end of our visit, my then three-year-old little sister hatched a plan to make it last longer! She broke away from me and ran over to where she saw a show taking place for children ages seven to eleven with clowns and balloons. When I went after her, she ran away from one of the clowns to Ms. Brooks. I walked over to where she was and picked her up. She had the most adorable smile on her little face, and I tickled her as we walked out of the chapel.

When we got back to my mother, Jarmal, and Ms. Imani, who was the caseworker, I tried to hand Ireena over to Jarmal, but Ireena made a little face that said she didn't like that at all. When Jarmal put her down, she broke away from him and ran away from him. I knew this wasn't going to be easy. I picked her up again and walked with them around the corner. When we got to the entrance, I couldn't go any further, so I again handed her to Jarmal. She looked over his shoulder and saw that I wasn't moving, which made my heart sink! She went into a frenzy, crying and trying to reach me over his shoulders with both hands. I couldn't do anything about it. After they walked through the door, I could still hear Ireena crying and shouting for me, but this time I couldn't rescue her. Mrs. Imani said, "You know, she really loves you." And I knew that was the truth!

My last week at Audy Home, I had a host of parties. Mrs. Adams gave me one; Mrs. Imani gave me one; Mr. Young did too; and so did Mr. Space. The last party was from Mr. Hedges. I had days at that place that I will never forget. Some of the happiest moments of my life were there. My birthday fell on a Sunday, and Monday was Columbus Day, so I left the Audy Home for Cook County Jail the day after that.

I arrived at the Cook County Jail on October 15. It was scary and unpleasant going through processing – the finger printing, strip search, and the STD testing. Jail was totally different from the Audy Home. After about five hours, I found out that they were sending me to Super-Max Division 11, Gallery D-B, and the first person I met there was a Traveler Vice Lord named My-My. He was very helpful, orienting me and helping me to keep out of trouble. I also met an old man named "Papa G" who showed me how to gamble. This helped me come up with enough money for food and toiletries.

Every month I went to court, but my lawyer didn't seem to really care. I wondered if telling her the truth would have made a difference. Yet, I figured it was better to be known as a killer than as someone who had been molested. *I'm going to die with this secret*, I thought to myself, and that was that.

The county jail was very scary, and I got very tired of being there. So much happened to me there that I couldn't put it all down here from just the year and a half that I was there. I knew that I was guilty and that I wasn't going home, so I took a plea bargain on July 14, 1998. My plea bargain brought my sentence down from eighty years to thirty-eight. Half of that would be nineteen years.

After I took the plea bargain, I was able to talk to my mother and Rodent, and I had a good visit with them, but then I realized that I was about to go to prison for nineteen years of my life. I remembered when Rodent used to tell me that, if I went to prison, they would probably send me to Pontiac Correctional Center, and I would run into a guy named Big Spicey, whom he warned me about. Now I was on my way to prison, and I was angry with them, though I didn't let on. I was indeed guilty, but I wished that they could have protected me somehow. Yet, the responsibility for the bad choices were my own.

They falsely accused me of robbing his house, but what else would they think when I went to his house with companions whose only reason to go there was to steal belongings? I did indeed steal his car – even though I turned it over to my companions. It may be true that Ishmael perjured herself in not having seen me in the car after the crime, but I did drive it. What I did was wrong – absolutely wrong. Because I didn't trust anyone, I never told anyone that James had molested me, nor that he had threatened Ireena and my life.

I sat in Cook County for two more weeks before I was transferred. I was the only eighteen-year-old kid going to Joliet Correctional Center. They handcuffed my wrists and ankles, and there was a chain around my waist connected to the handcuffs and ankle cuffs. They hurt. Once again I was about to start a new chapter in my life. Oddly, it seemed like a very short bus ride to Joliet Prison, but I imagine it was because I dreaded it so. I know that I surely wasn't ready to walk through those doors!

If you read the transcript of the proceedings, you might think that I am a really bad person, and your appraisal would be justified in light of what I did. Yet, somehow Judge Suria knew that something was wrong. He wanted to know why I pulled the trigger. Yet, because I was ashamed to tell what James had done to me, I merely told him what the public defender gave me to say. If you hate me, hate me for not telling the truth.

A Misguided Child

A misguided child comes to the penitentiary a rage-driven teenager
    He doesn't see that what life will be – its fear and constant danger.

Surrounded by bars of solid steel and three walls made of brick,
    The child still doesn't understand his situation's not a trick.

Eighteen hours of isolation the child passes every day,
    And still he dreams of getting out without consequences to pay.

The child thinks he's grown because he's in prison now,
    He hasn't yet mastered the rules and regulations to even go to chow.

The child stares at the ceiling gathering wild, impractical thoughts,
    Still in disbelief that he was ever caught.

Telling all his "war" stories involving his next to kin,
    He can't get away from his bleak dungeon.

Abandoned on the outside, the child feels all alone,
    Mad at the world when no one answers the telephone.

Punching at the cell's wall, he hurts no one but himself,
    The pain is but a reminder of being put upon a shelf.

The child forgets his outdate, acts as if he doesn't care,
    Facing many kinds of problems that a child was not meant to bear.

The child gives a frowny face to others so they'll think that he is mean,
    As the child pretends within himself that this is one bad dream.

The child was given time to serve, he's already done a bit,
    Compared to all the others, he is a lone misfit!

The child received from a so-called friend a rod to serve as a knife,
    He killed someone, now look at him – the child is serving life!

Chapter 15
A Misguided Child

"Freedom is an elusive concept, some men hold themselves prisoners even when they have the power to do as they please and go where they choose, while others are free in their heart, even as shackles restrain them."

– Frank Herbert

Every day in prison is just a regular, routine day. You wake up and eat breakfast at 4:30 a.m. Lunch is served at around 10:30 a.m., and dinner is around 3:00 p.m. After that comes recreation period to do whatever is available, depending on the prison. Aside from that, a prisoner can read or he can watch TV. If there is a day room where everyone can meet, prisoners can play cards. Lots and lots of time passes doing these same boring activities. Not much to look forward to with nineteen years to serve!

Entering the Joliet Correction Center with my Bible and pictures, I went through the whole ordeal of processing again – the fingerprinting, the strip search, the ID picture, noting of tattoos. Then I had to go to Internal Affairs and Gang Intel because I had been in a gang, and finally I was sent to the gallery. I was in a cell by myself, and the guards called chow line, which meant that it was time to eat. We had to walk in a single file line, and that's when I saw Derrick Hardaway again. He was serving his sentence for murder.

Later on that night when they passed out mail, I received a calculation sheet of how much time I had to serve. When I looked at it, I was shocked and yelled to the officer. When he came back I told him there was a mistake and that my out-date was supposed to read 2014, not 2033! He said, "What are you telling me for? Write to the record's office."

I answered, "I just got here – what is the record's office?"

Then someone told me how to fill out a request slip, which I did, informing them of the error. Another inmate told me that I had thirty days to revoke my plea, which meant I had only two weeks left to make the change. I needed help, and I needed it fast! Unfortunately, two days later I was transferred to Pontiac Correctional Center.

When I got to Pontiac, I had to go through orientation all over again, and I didn't have time to waste. I needed help because I didn't want to be stuck in prison all those extra years. I hadn't accepted such a long sentence in my plea bargain. Yet, thank God, in a couple of days our wing was allowed to go to the library, and I didn't waste any time talking to as many library law clerks as they had. One didn't want to help, but another helped me out. All he asked me for was my case number, and he filed the motion for me, and I paid for the shipping and postage. For my application to be valid, I had to revoke my plea. I called Rodent and told him that they had my outdate as 9-10-2033, and that he needed to get in contact with the public defender and revoke my plea. I found out later that he never did anything about it. Nineteen extra years in prison – why wouldn't they help their son?

After the law clerk filed my motion to get me back into court, there was nothing that I could do but wait and pray that I could get back into court. After a week, I heard nothing, and I was transferred to South lower, which was the only population incarceration left. I had a cell to myself, and all I could do was read and look at the wall. My neighbor used to send me cigarettes to help keep me calm. Suddenly they called "Yard!" We all went outside, and a 6'6", 300-pound guy walked up to me and asked me if I was in a gang. I told him I was a CVL, and he said that he was too, and that he was going to take me back to the brothers. I went over with him and met Phatan, one of leaders within the gang, and he looked at me and said, "What's up?" And since the big guy had already told him that I was a CVL, Phatan told me to walk with him, and he introduced himself and his rank. He told me quite plainly to stay away from the big guy who had just brought me over to him. I asked him what the big guy's name was, and he said, "Big Spicey." He was the guy that Rodent told me I would meet if I went to Pontiac. I already knew about "Big Spicy" and his history of knocking people out and raping them. I talked to Phatan a little more, then I made a call to Rodent and told him that I had met Big Spicy and that I was staying away from him! In that call I also found out that neither my mother or Rodent had called the public defender to get me back into court!

On August 24 at 9:00 p.m. I was awakened by Lt. Mrs. Jordan who asked me my name as she looked at a picture of me in her hand, then she asked me my ID number. After I told her, she said that my judge wanted me back in court the next day! I couldn't have been happier! She let me take a shower and told me that correctional officers would come to get me at 6:00 a.m.

In the morning two correctional officers came and gave me a white dress shirt and black pants. Again they handcuffed my wrists and ankles, processed me and put me in a van, then drove me to the court that was about a two – to three-hour

Chapter 15 *A Misguided Child*

drive away. I spent the trip watching the drivers of the other cars going by.

When I got to the courthouse, I was taken upstairs where the jury would be, and I met my public defender. She wanted to know why I revoked my plea. To be honest, I didn't know what the law clerk had done or what motion he had filed for me to get me back into court so quickly. He was the reason I was back in court to talk to my public defender. What I did know was that my outdate was wrong and that the year 2033 was *not* the year I was to be released. I showed her the calculation sheet they gave me, and she quickly recognized that it was wrong. When I went out before the judge, the public defender explained to him that I was under the old law that required that I only do 50 percent of my sentence. I was not under the Truth in Sentencing Act under which the convicted has to serve out 100 percent of his sentence, because the act was passed on August 20, 1995, and my crime was committed on August 16, 1995 – four days before the 100 percent law was passed. Then she and the judge sent memos and orders to correct my mettimus, and I left to go back to the Pontiac Correctional Center.

When I arrived back at Pontiac, I was very happy, even though I still had sixteen more years to serve. One thing that brightened my days was receiving my first letter there. It was from Mr. Hedges at the Audy House. He told me of the concern he and his wife had for me and my welfare, and he promised to send me some books. He was the one who introduced me to the author James Patterson so that I was able to check out his books from the prison library. Patterson became my favorite author.

When I was serving my time there, we could go to the yard an hour each day, and we could shower twice a week. They served us breakfast, lunch, and dinner in our cell, and that was it for twenty-three hours a day. Being in my cell for twenty-three hours each day caused me to sleep a lot because there wasn't much to do except read, and I could read, in one day, the two books I'd checked out of the library. Then it would be two more weeks until I could order more books. Reading and comprehension of what I read were hard for me. I couldn't figure out the mystery or the plot, and some chapters were just too long to hold my attention. I would read them though because there was nothing else to do.

My second letter came from my friend Carolynn. I was glad to hear from her. I didn't go outside much, and when I did, I played basketball. I wanted to stay away from the Conservative Vice Lords.

This routine went on daily for three months, and I was really debating going into protective custody because they had advantages over sitting around bored in the cell. Then an officer told me they were transferring everyone out because they were making the entire prison protective custody and segregation. This made me mad because I was comfortable the way I was, and I didn't have to see anybody, and I liked it that way. The following week I was transferred to Stateville Correctional Center.

In October of 1998 I arrived at

Stateville Correctional Center, went through receiving and orientation again, and was housed in East House on 5 Gallery. After being there two weeks, my mother sent me $300.00 to get everything I needed, then I received another $100.00 and a Bible that I hadn't asked for from Father Ron at Cook County Jail, and another $50.00 from Mr. Hedges. With all that money I bought a TV, a radio, blue jeans, toiletries, and some food. After I'd gotten everything I needed, there was nothing left to do but sit in my cell and watch TV. One day I was called to take my TABE test, which stands for Testing Adult Basic Education. I really didn't want to pass, so I failed on purpose so that I could go to school. As I lay in my cell vegetating, our shower day came up, and they jammed twenty-five of us into the shower with a sentry watching so that nothing happened while we were taking our shower. When we all went to eat, the Vice Lords were at the end of the line. That put many of us on high alert in case of a riot.

One day we were served pork at chow, and one of the Vice Lords ate it, which put him under violation by his fellow gang members. When we went to the yard the next day, some brothers were going to stab him, and another brother and I were to throw the knives over the wall. I had only been in prison for about two months! I prayed that night to God and to His beloved Son Jesus to help me. It was crazy being a Vice Lord because that meant being a Muslim, and Muslims don't eat pork. I didn't want a prison murder charge hanging over me along with my own murder charge. The men who had committed prison murders were serving life sentences, so they didn't care if they killed another person. However, I planned to get out. Besides, I wondered why they would want to kill a man just because he ate a pork chop. That was just crazy! This place was certainly nothing like Audy Home or the county jail. These guys were lost and scary.

Early the next morning God answered my prayer. There was suddenly a lockdown that lasted about four months! When there is a lockdown, prisoners don't go anywhere. Breakfast, lunch, and dinner come directly to your cell, and you get a shower maybe once a week. You have to take spot baths in the sink and wash all your clothes in a correspondence box that is only two feet by two feet. When lockdown was over, three of the Latin Kings hit a correction's officer and beat him pretty badly. I never even made it out of my cell before we were back on lockdown! I really did not mind. I found out later that the gang hit was off because the guy who ate the pork ran to protective custody, a very smart move. I would have gone myself to keep from being killed. More than anything, I wanted to go home!

During the time that we were on lockdown, I started picking up my Bible for something to read. When I did, I recalled a time when I was in Cook County Jail that my co-defendant Deveron quoted a Bible verse. I remembered him saying, "I am the way, the truth, and the life." I looked for hours for that line, then I looked in the concordance in the back of the Bible and found it in the

Chapter 15 *A Misguided Child*

book of John, chapter 14. For three hours I worked on memorizing all the scriptures from verse 1 to verse 11. Those were the first Bible verses that I ever learned by heart – even before the Lord's prayer and Psalm 23. This excited me so much that I went flipping through the Bible and came across Isaiah 9. I liked it so much that I memorized verses 2 through 71. Even after doing all that, I still wasn't ready to follow the Lord. I put my Bible down and let it collect dust, and then I continued my life as it had been.

I got a little surprise after being in East House about five months – my cellmate and I were in a random shakedown. We were both handcuffed to the rail, and an officer went through all our things. I can't say the correctional officer's name, but when he was done, he took me down to the sergeant's office and asked me about a certain picture I had. It was a picture of Rodent with about twenty other men who were all Freemasons from the St. Paul Grand Lodge. He asked me what I knew about this picture, and I told him that my stepfather was in it. He asked me to show him the picture and immediately said to me, "You are Brother Wash's son?" They called Rodent "Wash" for short because his last name is Washington. I said I was. He told me he knew Rodent and that he was a Mason from Prince Hall Lodge. We talked briefly, and I told him that I wanted out of this prison. The problem was that the correctional officer worked midnight shift, and he was assigned to H-House, which was protective custody. I was skeptical about going back there, but I knew he couldn't help me unless I did.

About three weeks later, I told them that I thought my life was in danger because I wanted to get out of the gang. They left me in protective custody holding, making sure that I was not going there to hurt anyone. After two weeks I was cleared to stay. They put me on the top floor in a cell by myself, and, oh, how I enjoyed this situation! Although I knew my life was going to be tough, it still would be better than it had been.

The correctional officer who asked me to come back there checked in on me to see if I was having any problems. I wasn't. He soon got me a job working in the kitchen, and I worked from 11:00 p.m. to 7:00 a.m. and was able to stay to myself. (My experience in cooking at home came in handy.) After a week or two, I was made cook, working in the officers' kitchen and making friends. Because I was cooking their food like they were at a restaurant, some of the officers would go to the vending machines and buy me cigarettes, pizza, and soda. Now I was doing well and was living pretty comfortably.

I remember one day I was frying the officers their chicken, and I was making a batter for the chicken. I saw a container of "all-purpose spice" and added about two cups of it to six cups of flour. After putting the chicken in the flour and then dipping it in the egg batter, I fried about forty breasts in four deep fryers. Then I started smelling something really sweet. The food supervisor smelled it and was wondering about it too. He tasted a piece of chicken and asked me why it tasted so sweet. I tasted a piece for myself and – wow – it *was* a little sweet! I looked at the seasoning bucket with "all-purpose spice" on it, and what I thought was garlic, onion powder, chili powder, and so on, turned out to be nutmeg, cinnamon, vanilla, and other spices for spice or carrot cake. To my surprise, it was crispy and it had a flavorful, sweet taste. Best of all, the officers liked it.

I went to work every day for about five months. I had been in Stateville for about eleven months when the correctional officer who had wanted me to come back there came to me and told me that I was on the transfer list to Illinois River Correctional Center. He told me that I needed to get away from the gangs and go to school. I wanted to do so, but it wouldn't be easy. Wednesday came, and I was transferred to Illinois River.

At Illinois River I went through orientation and receiving and was sent down to 4A where I knew a couple of my gang brothers, and, instantly, I was back into the gang. I ran into Phatan and told him that I wanted to fall back and get my life together, and he was happy with that. I didn't know that I wasn't a CVL anymore, so I thought that I had permission to stay in it. I continued doing CVL business. Phatan never really said what he was thinking, so I didn't know that, in his eyes, I was supposed to have dropped out of the gang. I would find out later what he thought. Without warning, I got moved down to 2B, where I saw two of my childhood friends – my best friends Kelvin and Taz – and then I found out that my co-defendant, Tyrice Reyes, was on 2A. I acted as if nothing were wrong, but I was still angry at him for taking a plea bargain of twenty years to testify against me. Still, I didn't bother him.

I noticed Kelvin was going to school and was taking computer technology, and I liked that. About three weeks later I was in Adult Basic Education because I needed to get my TABE test score above 6.0 from where I then was at 3.5. My teacher, Mrs. Tina Wierson, was a good person, and she worked with me until I understood what I needed to know to pass my GED. About three months later, I was applying myself in a GED class, and my scores were rising, and I was learning. I didn't realize that I was good at it. Of course, when everything is going well, someone will always try to tear you down. This time it was my co-defendant, Tyrice Reyes! He was going around telling all the Vice Lords that I had told on him, when he was the one who had told on me. Whatever anyone knew about him came from him. I never told anyone in the prison what he had done. He must have figured that I was about to tell on him, so he tried to beat me to it.

A meeting of all Vice Lords was called in the yard, and it was just one big argument about who told on who, and none of it could be proven. Therefore, they let it go. The next morning Tyrice Reyes was no longer in the prison. He had simply vanished!

In the meantime, I was finishing school and getting ready to take the GED test in a couple of months when I got called to the yard by Phatan about whether I was in the Vice Lords or not. I couldn't say that I wasn't when I had been in all of their business. Phatan was under the impression that I had dropped my flag when I had talked to him about it, and he accepted it. Now he was angry and wanted to beat

Chapter 15   *A Misguided Child*

me up, but he gave me an order to violate one of the brothers. I was to hit him twice in the mouth for talking crazy.

As I mentioned before, the CVL gang is Muslim, and Muslims don't eat pork. Members were required to give a "statement of love," which is a statement showing love and loyalty to the brothers in the gang. In reality, there was no love or loyalty for each other. As Muslims, they also had to pray to the East with their palms up, facing toward the holy city of Mecca. Although I wasn't a Muslim, I complied with their requirements to be a part of the gang. Yet, it really meant nothing to me.

The day came, and I had three Vice Lords with me in a room to violate the offending brother. After we vowed allegiance to our gang literature and prayed to the East, it was time to hit the guy in the mouth twice. I felt bad for him, but if I didn't hit him hard, I would get his violation. This guy just wouldn't stop talking, and he had only about seven teeth in his mouth now, but he just wouldn't stop talking, so I asked him if he was ready. This talker started talking tough about how small I was, and how I couldn't hurt him, so while he was talking, I punched him in the mouth and knocked his tooth out. When he got his composure together, he knew we were serious, and I punched him in the mouth again, and we left the cell and went separate ways on the wing.

My cellmate was a Conservative Vice Lord named Red who told me after this incident that I needed to lay low and give the mob up and stop gangbanging because all I did that day was create an enemy, and in the future if I should ever run into the guy whose tooth I had knocked out, there would be no love for me and he'd probably kill me. Red opened my eyes to start heading out of the mob.

After being in Illinois River about a year and a half, I was doing well and was about to get permission from Red to drop my gang flag. It seems contradictory that, when I was moved to 3A, they told me I was too young to get out and that I should not be able to get out because of Rodent's connection to the CVL. However, a guy named "Bone," who didn't know Rodent or his history with CVL said that I was going to have to get "violated out"! But I wasn't going to let that happen! I took a plastic coat hanger and made four knives out of them, hiding them around my waist in front and back. When the Vice Lords tried a sneak attack on me, I pulled out the knives and chased them away and then went back to my cell. The older man who was my cellmate came in and told me to give him the knives before the officers arrived. Less than two minutes later, five officers were at my door. They cuffed me and locked me up under investigation, but there was no evidence upon which to take action. I told them that I wanted out of this prison because I wanted out of the Vice Lords. The officers didn't believe me. I stayed in the hole for thirty days and then was put in a van with a disciplinary transfer to Pinckneyville Correctional Center. I could live with that. It was time for a new start. No more gangbanging. I wanted to change my life and find Jesus.

A Prisoner's Prayer

Heavenly Father,
    I am not so good at praying, why, I don't know how to pray;
   . I guess it's that I fear You and I don't know what to say.

Heavenly Father,
    Praying is more complicated than anything I've faced in my years!
    It's not as easy as watching TV or as painful as shedding tears.

Heavenly Father,
    For hours I've made the effort to pray like a deacon at church,
    How can I pray, when profane words won't do? I stumble in my search.

Heavenly Father,
    I will bow my head and pray the best I can, please forgive me when I intrude,
    And I plead for heavenly wisdom that my words to You are not rude.

Heavenly Father,
    I try not to cry as I go to sleep,
    I thought that it showed me to be weak.

Heavenly Father,
    I've tried so hard to forget the thoughts piled up inside my heart and my soul,
    But it's hard to let go of what got me here; the feelings have not grown cold.

Heavenly Father,
    It hurts sitting in a cell just gathering thoughts beyond my wildest imagination,
    Though my thoughts bring pain, they can build
    me up when I rise from the revelation.

Heavenly Father,
    Doesn't anyone understand that I've become a changed man.
    They see me as a hardened killer, and not who I am through Your plan.

Heavenly Father,
    So I close my prayer with happy heart and soul,
    I've poured out my heart, and my story's now been told.

Chapter 16
A Prisoner's Prayer

"If we show that the way of righteousness is also the way of happiness, then even the hardest of criminals will be eager to follow it."

– John Chrysostom

When I got to Pinckneyville Correction Center, I saw that an inmate does pretty much the same thing every day, day after day. Then he wakes up and does it all over again. However, this time when I arrived, I had a plan in my head, and I believed I was making the right decision in no longer claiming or acknowledging CVL. At this new place I was going to go to school and get my life right and find God. Unfortunately, since I didn't have any money coming in on a regular basis, I played poker every day for income. After being there for two months doing nothing, I was called over to the academic building and asked if I wanted to take a GED class. I did, I really did! I started thinking about all the teachers who told me that I wouldn't amount to anything, and I said to myself, *I may be in prison, but I am not dead!*

Let's do it!

When I started school, I went full force. I studied long and hard and was pretty good at everything except reading and writing. Math came very easy to me, but I had a hard time comprehending the things I read. I would try to read, but it was as if the information just didn't sink in. I told Mr. Hedges about this, and he started sending me James Patterson novels. Those books caught my attention and enabled me to begin storing information and comprehending what I was reading. That one skill helped me so much as I continued my schooling.

When it was time for me to take my GED, I passed it the first time. I was so pleased, even though I just barely passed writing skills, interpreting literature, and arts. Nonetheless, I thank God that I passed!

Around April 2001 I finished school and got a job working for Lt. Jordan on inside grounds mowing the grass. She had transferred from Pontiac Correction Center. As I worked, I watched a guy working with flowers, and I told Lt. Jordan that I would like to try that job too. I found out that those who worked in landscaping were part of a horticulture class. So, I had to get on a waiting list for that when I was already on a waiting list to take computer technology. I was inspired to look into computer technology by my friend Kelvin. I wanted to follow in his footsteps because people had also told him that he would amount to nothing, and it was time that we both showed those people that they were wrong!

One day as I was out mowing grass behind Cell Houses 1 and 2 beside the fence, I was enjoying the beautiful sight on the other side of those gates. As I was mowing along, I hit what I thought was a patch of grass, and suddenly, a cloud of grasshoppers flew into the air. It must have been a nest of some kind. You would have thought that I was being struck by God and that He had sent out the eighth plague, there were so many of them. I took off running toward Cell House 4 and completely forgot that I was in a no-run zone – I was so scared! I ran behind the eell house and ran right beside the fence. I stopped by a cell room window and was frightened again by what I saw – a huge black and yellow spider in the window. The body of the spider was the size of a human thumb, and its legs were about an inch to an inch and a half. It scared me so much that I backed up and tripped over my own feet. I then walked quickly back to my lawnmower. I didn't quite make it to the tower because someone reported my running. Of course, they didn't say that I had been running away from a plague of locusts or a man-eating spider. It just looked like I was trying to escape.

Officers came out of nowhere in a hurry! There must have been about twenty strong men coming from every direction. They forced me to the ground and were about to walk me to segregation, but thanks to Lt. Jordan, I was able to show them the plague of grasshoppers and the "man-eating" spider, and they called me a scaredy-cat, but let me go. Then they changed my job to just picking up trash dropped on the ground. I worked from 8:00 a.m. to 2:30 p.m., but that was just fine. It was better than going to segregation or getting charged with an attempted escape! I enjoyed working outside all day.

On September 11, 2001 – the famous 9/11 day in history – I woke up around 8:00 a.m. and saw that I was late, so I turned on my TV and was watching the news when I saw that a plane had crashed into the World Trade Center in New York. It was breaking news on every channel! I watched it for a while, but knew I had to get outside to work before 9:00 a.m. In a few minutes, I saw a second plane on the news crash right into the second building. Then the news went from saying it was breaking news to saying America was under attack, and I felt sad, hurt, and mad, wondering who did it and how dare they attack my home country! I woke my roommate up and told him to watch the news while I went out to

Chapter 16 *A Prisoner's Prayer*

work. While I was out there, I heard over the officers' walkie talkies that the first tower had collapsed, and I thought about all those innocent people dying for just going to work! Then I was standing next to Lt. Jordan when I heard that the second building collapsed too, and I just felt overwhelmed with sorrow and anger. We just all stood there in front of the dietary building in silence because in our hearts we just couldn't believe that we were being attacked. The next instant a lady came running out of the administration building yelling and crying, "They hit the Pentagon! They hit the Pentagon!"

I looked at Lt. Mrs. Jordan and said, "We're about to go into lockdown. They just took out our defense system."

Then Lt. Mrs. Jordan got a call to go and get someone and put him in segregation for his own protection. They went through the entire prison and put everyone who was of Arab descent into segregation, even though half of them were born in the United States! But the prisoners wouldn't know that, and I think this was a smart call from the prison administration. I told the officer in charge that I was going in, and I went and took a shower. Before I went in, I grabbed my radio from an associate who was a couple cells down from mine. I didn't want to go on lockdown without my radio – especially not knowing at the time how long lockdown would be. We stayed on lockdown for a couple of days, and I watched the news all day long. Later on, I found out that a lot of people died in the second tower because they were sent back to work after the first tower was hit. I wanted so bad to join the Army, but my being in prison kept me from getting caught up in someone's political agenda. It was one of the saddest times in my incarceration.

About a month later, I got a call from the college coordinator for Rend Lake College asking me if I wanted to take a computer technology class. When I got there, I was introduced to my instructor Mrs. Nancy Woods, who put me on computer #16. I learned quickly! I don't know how it happened, but Mrs. Woods and I developed a type of mother-son relationship. I took computer technology tech math and was getting it! But I was failing, and failing miserably, at one section. However, Mrs. Woods would not give me a final grade. I must have done that section over and over again about five times. Every time I would get a D, yet she was not recording it. Instead, she would just send me to the back of the class away from the computers and other students. I thought she was picking on me. I was so tired of repeating that chapter that I pushed the book away from me and told Mrs. Woods that I quit the class.

She looked at me for a while, turned back around, typed a little on her computer, then turned around and quietly walked up to me, leaned over my table, and said in a quiet voice, "You can't quit. These guys behind me – they can quit. You can't. Now, stop pouting and do your work."

And she pushed the book back in front of me. Now this made me furious so I announced, "I said I ain't doin' nothin'! I don't care what you do!"

She walked to the back and said, "Guess what! I don't care! Your problem is that you are too stubborn to ask for help. You think you can do everything!" Then she left. At that point, I didn't know what to do. The guys around me told me to not show up for class and she wouldn't have any choice but to drop me from the class. Yet, I couldn't do that to myself, and for some reason, I kept going back every day. I didn't say anything to Mrs. Woods for about three days. I would just sit in the back of the class and look mean all day. About the fourth day, I said "good morning" to her, but she didn't even acknowledge me – not a word! It bothered me that my lack of caring had made her that angry at me.

The following week, I went in, apologized to Mrs. Woods, and asked her for help. She accepted my apology, and with her help, I passed computer technology tech math with an overall grade of a "B." She moved my computer now from #16 to #1 – right by her desk, and I finished the class with a GPA of 3.4. That was five A's and eight B's. When I was done, she let me stay in the class and help her decorate. In January 2002 Rend Lake College pulled out of the prison while I was enrolled in an advanced computer class. Two weeks later they renewed their contract with the prison and came back. Almost losing the college contract with the prison made me appreciate the education I was getting, and it made me glad that I had enrolled.

Because I wanted to work in the prison industry where I could make about $200.00 a month, I put in for a transfer to Graham Correction Center. I got it, and enjoyed amazing freedom at Graham. I was out of my cell all day. Yet, there was a downside – seeing some money and getting a job in prison industry made me forget all about my plan to get my life together with God. For about five months, all I did was play poker on the wing – from 7:30 a.m. until 9:00 p.m.

One of those days we were playing poker, and a guy named Ta-dow was losing really badly. He was in the hole about $150.00, so he started calling everyone at the table disrespectful names. I wasn't having it, and I told him, "You don't know me, so you have no right to disrespect me." That got us into a confrontation. My cellmate, "Snake," the biggest guy on the wing, heard the raucous and came out of his cell. Ta-dow called me into his cell to fight. I was 5'9" and 135 pounds; Ta-dow was 6'3" and 230 pounds. He had a major advantage, but I wasn't going to be a coward like the other guys. I walked into his cell, and he pretended that he was talking, and I thought that everything was fine. When I started to leave, he called me. As I turned around, he hit me right square on the nose! The blow was so hard that everything went black with yellow stars and birds singing! It took me a second to regain my composure, but when I did, I flew at him with a flurry of punches. Even though I am not that strong, I am quick and accurate. Nonetheless, in the end, he beat me up all over that cell, and I was locked in! Thank God my cellmate went out and got Ta-dow's cellmate's key and pulled me out.

As I walked out, I defiantly declared, "You just beat me up, but you're still a no count!" I had two black eyes and a busted

Chapter 16 *A Prisoner's Prayer*

nose, and "Snake" was mad because he knew that Ta-dow was just a bully. When he went to fight Ta-dow, Ta-dow wouldn't fight him, like the true coward that he was. That experience taught me how dangerous it was to fight inside someone's cell. I might have died if Snake hadn't come. Why did I get in it at all? It was because I wanted to prove that I was not a coward when he called me a name – a name that could have cost me my life! We never got in trouble for that fight, and I never told on him. However, one day the police did a raid on the poker game and walked everyone at the table to segregation – everyone, that is, but me, because my wounds were still healing from the fight with Ta-dow. See how good God was in coming at different times to my rescue!

Then I got the call to work in the prison industry where they make college furniture for dormitories. I would work as a porter, starting out making $60.00 a month. However, I ran into conflicts with the workers. They reported everything I did or didn't do, like failing to sweep part of the floor near their area. I made the mistake of thinking that I was doing so well that I didn't need other people, but this experience showed me I always needed God and that I should not think too highly of myself.

After working there a month, I got into an argument with a lieutenant correctional officer who called me a "boy." I reacted poorly to him and spouted some words. I went right to segregation and was transferred to Lawrence Correctional Center.

At Lawrence Correctional Center I had to start over again with the usual orientation and intake preliminaries. The difference at Lawrence was that an inmate is locked up in his cell almost twenty-four hours a day. Not much happened there.

It was in 2004 that I felt Jesus really trying to get a hold of me. My cellmate's name was something like "Tone." A Christian, he used to study and read his Bible all day and write letters. In his correspondence box, I saw five yellow books. Taking a closer look, I saw that the one on top was *Patriarchs and Prophets* by Ellen G. White. Wondering what it was about, since I did like to read, I asked him to tell me about the book. He told me that he would respond after I first answered a few questions. I thought that was fair enough. His first question was: "What was the fruit that Adam and Eve ate in the Garden of Eden?"

I responded: "An apple."

"Wrong," he said. The next question was: "How many wise men were at the birth of Jesus?"

I answered: "Three."

Again he said, "Wrong." He then asked me, "When is the Sabbath?"

And I asked him what he meant by that, for I was not familiar with the word. He explained that it was the day set aside by God for us to worship Christ on.

I answered "Sunday," and again I was wrong. Then he went to the Bible and showed me, according to Scripture, why I was wrong in each case. The Bible doesn't identify what kind of fruit came from the tree of knowledge of good and evil. The idea that there were three kings is based on the number of gifts they brought. I asked him why he studied so hard, and he said "to show himself approved" or something like that, which I found out later is a Bible verse in 2 Timothy, chapter 2, verse 15. I did not understand all that he was telling me, and I was really surprised when he told me that he was a Seventh-day Adventist Christian.

Immediately my mind went back to my childhood and the people that I saw going to church on Saturday and the sign that said "Seventh-day Adventist." I wanted to hear more about what the name meant. He told me that the true Bible Sabbath is kept on the *seventh day* or Saturday. Then, he said, the word "Adventist" refers to the advent, or second coming, of Jesus. Adventists believe Jesus' advent is coming soon. So did I. That is what caused me to want to study about the Seventh-day Adventists.

The Seventh-day Adventist faith was interesting and enlightening, and I wanted to know all I could about it, so I wrote Mrs. Miriam Hedges at the Audy Home, and we talked about it. I asked her for the five volumes of "The Conflict of Ages" series by Ellen G. White. These were the yellow books that Tone had in his box. I was surprised to find out that her father was a Seventh-day Adventist pastor and that her sister was also a Seventh-day Adventist! The Hedges were kind enough to buy me the five books – *Patriarchs and Prophets*, *Prophets and Kings*, *The Desire of Ages*, *The Acts of the Apostles*, and *The Great Controversy* – and I enjoyed them very much.

Being in the cell with Tone was very relaxing. He showed me how to break away from traditional church Bible study and how to seek and study for myself. I didn't like bothering him when he was studying, but he was a peaceful and prayerful person. He used to pray for me. At the time, I really didn't know how to pray and was a little embarrassed to try. I was still in the process of transitioning into a new, hopefully better character. After a month my new cellmate was moved, and I again lost focus on my spiritual life.

About that same time, I remember receiving a letter while I was in my cell that was from my mother. In it she told me about Jarmal's enlistment in the Army. I thought that was a good thing for him because he would finally be doing something with his life. During his three months of basic training, he wrote me letters telling me how he hated the way that we were raised and that he would be sending me $50.00 every week. I think Rodent kept one or two of them since Jarmal could send letters to me, but he had to send a check to Rodent, and Rodent would make out a money order and send it to me. Sometimes I wouldn't get a money order, so I figured Rodent must have thought he needed it more than I did. These letters between Jarmal and me were the only line of communication I had with him, and he surely vented some angry, hateful feelings toward our parents. I thought I was angry at them, but I could see that, compared to Jarmal's anger, mine was like a drop of water in a pond. Jarmal was furious!

After three months I stopped hearing from him, which really puzzled me. My mother wrote me saying that Jarmal had gone crazy and went AWOL, which means he took off without telling anyone and left the Army, which is considered a crime. My mother went on to explain that, within a short period of time, two of my close friends were murdered. Demar Buffin had been incarcerated at either Sheridan Correctional Center or Shawnee Correctional Center and that, when he was released on a Friday, the following day he was driving around with Ahmad when a guy ran up to the car and shot three times into the car, hitting Demar three times in the stomach.

My heart fell to the floor! I couldn't believe it! The "Little Beast" was gone – and for what? Then, as I continued reading, my mother told me about Ahmad and how he had gone to see a girl and was parking his car when some guys suddenly ran up to his car and shot it up, hitting Ahmad about sixteen times, obviously killing him. I was so angry, so hurt, so broken, and so lost. In just one letter I had lost my brother, Demar, and Ahmad! Why? I figured that Jarmal couldn't handle their deaths and that that was probably why he left the Army as he did. In prison, death is dealt with differently. We have to deal with it as though it never happened. We have to put it behind us and move forward, and that's what I did.

After a while I was able to start taking classes for my associate's degree in general studies. That helped me take my mind off of all the things going wrong with my friends and family about which I could do nothing. The sense of helplessness in losing my best friends and my brother going missing was excruciating. In spite of everything, something good came out of it all – I stayed in school! That was probably the best thing I could do for myself at that time anyway.

Together with the associate's degree, I was allowed into the food service class, and the first teacher we had taught us how to cook from the menu. But she quit her job to marry a man making a six-figure salary. I really couldn't blame her. Soon we had another teacher named Mr. Cantu. He was a real chef, and "Chef" is what we called him. He didn't care much about bookwork. What was important to him was how the food we prepared looked and tasted. I did well at this. With everything that I learned, I realized that I was pretty smart and that *I could* amount to something, yet I wanted to learn more. I stayed at that prison for three and a half years. After I graduated with my associate's degree and my food service certificate, I requested a transfer to Big Muddy Correctional Center because I really wanted to take the construction class, and it was the only prison that offered it.

Go Read

Years ago my mind was lost and I didn't care about much, I committed
   a crime at the age of fifteen. Go read Exodus 20:13.

I had so many bad emotions. I was mentally, physically,
   emotionally, and spiritually sick! Go read Psalms 18:6.

I was guilty of my crime, no surprise when of my freedom
   I was deprived. Go read 1 Corinthians 4:3-5.

When I saw the light and wanted to make a change, I
   believed it was too late. Go read Acts 2:38.

Due to the nature of my crime, I'm frequently not accepted, and
   occasionally people are mean. Go read Colossians 3:13.

When I was humble, trouble came knocking at
   my door. Go read Mathew 5:44.

I tried to forget the past, what others and I did and
   what I had seen. Go read Philippians 3:13.

To some people I might not be forgiven, nothing more
   than gum on a shoe. Go read Ephesians 4:32.

I close my eyes in prayer, wishing I could be under
   a picturesque tree. Go read Psalm 23.

I believe in my heart that everlasting life is my part in the
   earth made new. Go read Revelation 21:1, 2.

If you don't know what I'm saying, still, try to
   remember me. Go read Hebrews 13:3.

Chapter 17
Go Read

"A general slain in battle is lost to his army, but his death gives no additional strength to the enemy. But when a man of prominence joins the opposing force, not only are his services lost, but those to whom he joins himself gain a decided advantage."

– Ellen G. White, *The Acts of the Apostles*

In the fall of 2007, I was transferred to Big Muddy River Correctional Center, and after the usual orientation, I put in for the construction class and was put on a waiting list. In the meantime I was doing my usual, poker playing, but I felt I was still changing for the better, though slowly. I looked at the chapel list, and didn't really see anything for special classes, so I didn't put in for anything there. Then I heard that, on Thursday night, Seventh-day Adventist Pastor Florin Liga would be coming. I put in for this to see what it was about. When I put in for the kitchen, I got that job pretty quickly. After forty-five days I was made a cook.

One day I was cooking Monte Cristo sandwiches for the kitchen workers when a friend of mine, Stan Stephens, wanted to take his food back to his cell with him with some dessert. It's forbidden to take any food out of the dietary area back to the cell, but I wasn't going to say anything since he had been doing it for months. They called him "Doc," for short, and he had only one hand, the other one had been badly burned in a warehouse electrical fire. I used to help him with what he couldn't do, and we became friends. He would hide his food. One time when the food supervisor, Mr. Johnson, had a shake down, he found some food in the dishroom that I had cooked and some bleach and liquid soap. He came back to the kitchen and yelled at me – with profanity – to get out of his kitchen. I looked at him kind of puzzled, not knowing what was going on yet, and he yelled at me again to get out of there. I walked out into the dining area and sat down. Then Doc came in and filled me in on what was going on. Even though the food that they found of Doc's wasn't mine, I still got blamed for it because the food supervisor knew that I was the one who cooked it and gave it out, making me ultimately responsible.

I couldn't and wouldn't tell on Doc, so I went directly to the food supervisor, Mr. Johnson, and told him the food was mine but that the bleach and soap were not. After that, every time he saw me, he would write out a disciplinary ticket against me for things that I didn't do! After receiving four tickets from him for things that I knew I did not do, I reported him for harassment and sent copies to the administration staff, internal affairs, the director, the deputy director, and anyone who had authority over the next person all the way to the top. Three days later they called me into internal affairs because they thought I was about to sue them. Of course, that wasn't what I intended, nor did I want Mr. Johnson to lose his job. I just didn't want to be punished for something I didn't do, and I wanted him to leave me alone. Lt. Mr. Shuler, who was over internal affairs, told me that he had reviewed my file, that I hadn't been in any major trouble, and that I had done a lot of schooling. He asked me why I was at that prison. I told him that I wanted to take construction, and he said that he would see what he could do. One week later I was called over to talk about taking construction, and I decided to sign up for it. I started the following week. I surely was glad to get away from that kitchen!

My new instructor was Mr. Duncan. His motto was: "Don't bother me. Direct all questions to my assistants." The problem was that the assistants didn't have the answers I needed, so I had to study very hard. When I got into my second book of blueprint reading, I really liked that class. However, I wasn't passing, and I knew that I should get it right before my final test. So, I went over all my past tests and discovered that there were questions that weren't in the current textbook but were in the earlier edition. My grade went from a C to a B by fixing the questions on the test. Mr. Duncan didn't like me caring about my GPA.

I finally got over to the chapel and met Pastor Florin Liga, the Seventh-day Adventist pastor. When I walked into the chapel and met him, he greeted everyone who came through the door. He had an accent, which we found out later was Romanian, and he was a kind and friendly man. Every class began with opening prayer and three songs out of a hymnbook. Pastor Liga taught out of the book of Daniel, which is known for its prophecies. Though I didn't understand prophecy or its importance for the world's future, for the first time in a long time I felt humbled in my spirit and at peace. I knew that I was now spiritually at home in the Seventh-day Adventist Church. I studied hard, and I noticed that the more I studied God's Word, the more the devil attacked my spiritual growth. Nonetheless, I held on.

Though I wasn't yet baptized, I considered myself a Seventh-day Adventist, and I was really happy to meet other

Chapter 17 *Go Read*

Seventh-day Adventists in the prison. As we studied, I came to the conclusion that I needed the *Seventh-day Adventist Bible Commentaries* for help in study, but I couldn't afford their $418.00 price tag. What was I to do? Pastor Liga suggested I talk with Brother Matthew for some ideas on how to get them. (We all called each other brother in his class. It is interesting that I once thought of gang members as brothers, and now my brothers were people who were seeking after God!)

When I talked to Brother Mathew Oliver, he had a great idea. He told me to write to thirty different churches and ask them each to donate $15.00 to the Adventist Book Center on my behalf for those books. He gave me all the addresses of the churches in Illinois. I asked Pastor Liga what he thought about the idea and he said he would call the store and tell them to be on the lookout for the money coming in so that Paul would know it was OK. However, there was only one problem! I was living on only $15.00 a month, and thirty envelopes with thirty stamps would cost me $15.00, and I was by now barely hearing from my own family except maybe once every four to six months. Money was scarce.

What could I do? I prayed and went back and talked to Doc about it, and the next time Doc came to see me a couple days later, he asked me if I still wanted those commentaries, and I said yes, and he dropped thirty pre-stamped envelopes on my bed and told me to get to writing – and that's just what I did! Was my prayer ever answered! I wrote by hand thirty letters to the thirty churches, but only a few responded. They were Belvidere Seventh-day Adventist Church, Stewardson Seventh-day Adventist Church, Freeport Seventh-day Adventist Church, New Hope Seventh-day Adventist Company, and Burbank Seventh-day Adventist Church. How disappointed I was that I didn't hear from all of them, but I prayed that our Lord would touch their hearts to help me.

A couple of months later I was surprised to receive the commentaries. I later learned that Paul Neat, the manager of the Adventist Book Center, had raised the rest of the money for them – what a blessing that was! I was learning now to pray about everything! "Don't worry about anything; instead, pray about everything; tell God your needs, and don't forget to thank him for his answers" (Philippians 4:6, TLB). I'm also happy to say that after attending his services for about four to six months, on June 26, 2008, I gave my life over to Christ and was baptized as a Seventh-day Adventist Christian.

We went on lockdown in Big Muddy River for some reason, and when we came out of it, I had to take four tests in plumbing, and four in masonry, and it would be seemingly impossible to take all of them in a four-day period because my time was up, and I had to move into my next class. I asked Mr. Duncan for an extension, but he said no. I told him I was going to fail or it was going to ruin my GPA.. He told me that he didn't care about me failing or about my GPA, so I went to my Lord in prayer, asking Him to help me get through it and to bring back to my memory all that I'd stored in it. Then I took all those tests and surprisingly passed two tests, failed one and barely passed the final and came out with two "C's" – the first two "C's" I had ever had in my college career. The best part was that I got a Rafter Math and Habitat for Humanity Certificate and my degree. I have to tell you that the reason I didn't do well on my test was that the whole time we were on lockdown I didn't touch my masonry or plumbing book. I was under the impression that when school resumed, we would just pick up where we left off, so I just used that time to study the Bible commentaries that I had recently gotten, and I learned about Bible history and archaeology. I enjoyed learning about ancient history.

Of all the thirty churches I wrote, Sister Shirley Dear from the Belvidere Seventh-day Adventist Church was the first to respond to my request. After her initial response, we began corresponding and became good friends. She sent me Bible studies on general topics and then on Daniel and Revelation. From this point on in my life, I went from having mail only every four to six months to having a letter every two weeks from Sister Shirley. She typed the letters in which she taught me the Word of God.

Connie Thompson from the Stewardson Seventh-day Adventist Church was the next person to write me. She was indeed another blessing from God. We also corresponded and soon became friends. After a while she wanted me to meet her daughter Joisha, and she and I soon became friends too. When I recognized that she had feelings for me, I thought it only proper that I let her mother know about it. She gave me her blessing to pursue a relationship with her daughter. It was the month of October, and it was going on ten years since I had had a visitor – October 21, 1998, was the last time I had a visit or saw my mother.

On October 27, 2008, I was called downstairs for their visit, and I couldn't believe it. They were here – my first visit in ten years! That day I met Joisha and Mrs. Connie, and we had a blast. Jesus was working in my life! We talked, laughed, and prayed together, and Joisha and I got along pretty well. She had such pretty eyes, and we visited for five hours. Two days later I got another visit from Joisha, and the next day too!

Then later on I got a visit with Joisha and her son, Bryante, and he became my little buddy. He was one of those kids that would make any father proud, and he had dreams of becoming a chef, so I thought I'd do something special for him since I had graduated from food service. He wanted a Le Cordon Bleu Cookbook for his birthday. When they came to visit me again, I gave little Bryante a copy of the cookbook that I got from my teacher, and he was the happiest kid you ever saw! By now Joisha was visiting me every week, and our relationship was getting serious.

On Thanksgiving Day of November 27, 2008 – the first Thanksgiving I had ever gotten a visit – Joisha and I began to talk about marriage, and she asked me to marry her. All I could think about was marrying her, but there were some problems. After our visit I asked the chaplain about marriage procedures, and he asked me if she had any children. I said yes, and

Chapter 17 *Go Read*

that I was incarcerated for murder. He then told me that he wouldn't approve of my marriage until I took anger management and parenting classes. That was all fine with me.

Soon I was back in school and finally taking the horticulture class. There was so much to learn about plants. My instructor, Mr. Gary, was the kind of teacher who didn't mind answering questions. He was my kind of teacher.

In December, just before Christmas, Pastor Liga handed out Bible-reading-in-a-year plans. That night I made my commitment to read the Bible in one year. On January 1, 2009, I started the daily readings.

After a while things began to change between Joisha and me. Instead of visiting me every week, Joisha's visits stretched to every two. On April 9, 2009, she introduced me to a good friend of her mother's, whose name was Debbie Weiland. The two ladies were like sisters. By now we were all so close that Mrs. Connie was calling me "son" and I was calling her "mom." Mrs. Weiland was a new blessing in my life. In fact, we got to know each other so well that I started calling her "auntie." She loved me and I loved her. I can't explain the joy she brought to me. All the love and attention I was getting from my new "family" made my incarceration much easier to bear. For nearly two years, I had had no personal property in my cell, like a fan or a TV, etc. All that I had were my textbooks, but now "Auntie Debbie" bought me a TV, gym shoes, and food. We also enjoyed studying the Bible together. I can never say how thankful I am for her being in my life. She blessed me in so many ways and made my time in prison more comfortable as I followed Jesus.

Over time Joisha introduced me to her other two kids, Cheyenne and Anthony, and to her grandmother Shirley and cousin Eric. She wrote me faithfully, and we would talk on the phone. However, she wasn't telling me everything that was going on.

By June of 2009 she was only coming up once a month, and I heard that she was steadily getting into arguments and fights with her mother. It seemed that Joisha didn't want to work, and when she got a job, she would quit it. I didn't give up on her, and I wrote her every other day. By now we had two new volunteers in the chapel, Pastor Steve Nelson and his wife, Samantha. Pastor Nelson was Joisha, Connie, and Debbie's pastor. He already knew how I felt about Joisha so we were getting ready to start pre-marriage counseling when I heard that she was living with a guy named Hollywood and that they were more than friends! I was crushed and didn't know what to do. The devil does indeed work harder in your life when he sees you following the Lord. He surely was trying to bring me down again.

I continued going to school and learning everything I could about flowers. I was also on the softball team because Aunt Debbie wanted me to play. It helped me keep my mind off Joisha. I am glad to say that at this time I was feeling happy and blessed that the Lord was looking down on me and answering my prayers. I prayed more, and I became a peacekeeper and Sabbathkeeper. I talked to other inmates about Christ – not to force religion on them, but to offer them something greater in life than what we had in prison – a better life with Christ in it. If they wanted to do a Bible study, I would refer them to Sister Shirley who always sent out Bible studies with her friendly letters. I soon found out that most men were more interested in a pen pal than in learning about the Lord. Still, a few of them did make good use of her Bible lessons! I noticed that, when a person is doing well in prison, the devil doesn't like it, so he tries to "upset the apple cart" in any way he can. *We are only safe in clinging to our Savior daily.* At that time, life was all right for me, so I wasn't all that worried about Joisha. I assumed that she would show up eventually. However, the devil was at work.

One night I went to chapel and Pastor Nelson told me that he was sorry. I didn't know what he was sorry about. Then I went to greet his wife, Sister Nelson, and she said that she was sorry too. Why was everybody so sorry? What was going on? Then Pastor Nelson asked me to go to the back so we could talk. I thought that someone had died, but, thank God, that was not the case. He quickly realized that I didn't know what he was talking about, and he asked me, "When was the last time you heard from your mom or Joisha?"

I said, "Mom, last month. Joisha two and a half months ago." He paused and then said that he hated to tell me, but that Joisha had been dating a guy named Rex for about two months and that they were about to get married. He refused to marry them. What pressure must have been on his shoulders to tell me! He couldn't have delivered anything much worse! In one way it was good because I wasn't left wondering anymore. Now I knew that she was gone for good. Unfortunately, when I knew that the relationship was definitely over, I lost control. I stopped caring about my progress and became angry. I had filed for clemency with the governor's office to increase my chances of an early release. Now my reason for filing was no more.

On the softball field, I got into an argument with another player, and when we went back to our cells, he tried to snake me. All the anger I had toward Joisha, I released in a fight. I beat the guy up and choked him enough that he blacked out. Fortunately, later he became my friend. After the fight I went back to school and studied harder, graduating from the horticulture class. I didn't have the motivation to enroll in any other classes there because, after things ended with Joisha, the memories of her visits were too painful. I left Big Muddy River Correctional Center and put in for a transfer to Centralia Correctional Center to take classes on drafting. I intended to make a new start in a new place.

On December 21, 2009, I completed the Bible reading in a year. There were days when I would be upset and would forget to read, and I would have to make it up, reading twice as much the next day. Yet, I kept at it, with determination and dedication to my Lord's words, "Man shall not live by bread alone, but by every word that proceedeth out of the mouth of God" (Matthew 4:4, KJV). I felt it was quite an accomplishment!

In May 2010 I arrived at Centralia Correctional Center and tried to sign up for drafting, but the drafting teacher had retired. It just so happened that I ran into Assistant Warden Hilliard, who had been the assistant warden at Big Muddy River Correctional Center. At Big Muddy River, he had a tropical flowering plant called a Dieffenbachia, or Dumbcane. It had been dying from the students' overwatering of it. He asked me to bring it back to health, which I was able to do. Now that he was at Centralia, I asked him if I could get a job in the greenhouse, and he said that he would take care of it.

It took until August, but I finally got the job, although I had to start off working in the garden first. Our job in that nice-sized garden was to keep it weeded and to pick the vegetables as needed. We took the vegetables to the prison dietary and to Mr. Pauly who was the teacher of the food service class. It was very hot some days, reaching over 100 degrees. I sometimes would hide in the cornfield, which wasn't a very good idea if you're scared of insects as I was. Everything in the garden was organic, and every morning I could eat fresh vegetables like tomatoes, cucumbers, cantaloupes, snap peas, green beans, watermelon, and bell peppers. Then when the garden died off in October, I was able to work in the greenhouse, which was a comfortable place to work.

I was told to bring something new to the plant sale at Centralia when I transferred because it was rumored that Big Muddy River Correctional Center had the best plant sale. The greenhouse at Centralia was very different from theirs. The greenhouse itself is smaller; there is only so much dirt, so many flower pots, hanging baskets, and cell packs; there is no fertilizer or peat moss, mulch, or even slow release flower fertilizer to help the plants grow. These factors made it tougher to grow healthy plants at Centralia, and it was our job to work with the seeds.

Around December I started germinating seeds and transplanting them. I did about 90 percent of all the plants. There were only two of us working, and the other guy was named Johnny Mellizas. We were always arguing about the plants because he wanted to do it his way, yet, because he hadn't taken the horticulture class, he really didn't know much about plants. We did agree on one thing though and that was that I would do the germinating, transplanting, and caring for the seedlings because Johnny watered too much! Together we were successful. I grew enough plants to have two plant sales and still be able to install plants around the whole prison! The Employee Benefit Fund for the Centralia staff invested $600.00 to buy what we needed: the dirt, the seeds, the cellpacks, the perlite, and the hanging baskets. We used all that and made a profit of about $1,100.00 in just a few days! After the plant sale, Johnny and I started taking care of all the flowerbeds around the prison, and later on, we became good friends.

I would take fresh cut flowers from the greenhouse to the ladies in the school staff, Mrs. Zahm and Mrs. Muggins, and to Mrs. Tina Wolfe, the assistant of Mr.

Evans, who was the college coordinator. Mrs. Wolfe is a great person who later was promoted to Mr. Evans' position. She showed me a lot of things to help prepare me for life outside prison, like how to budget my money, fill out checks, make bank statements, file my taxes, and so on. She cared when many people did not.

I started an electronics class on December 19, 2011, and it was probably one of the hardest classes I ever took in my entire life. Nonetheless, I worked hard at it for about eight weeks. I was close to getting through the class on direct current, when – out of the blue – I received a very negative letter from "Aunt" Debbie, and it crushed me! The things that she said to me in that letter hurt deeper than she'll ever know, and I knew the devil had gotten a hold of her somehow because this was not like her at all. I was so hurt that I couldn't focus on school, and I started failing. I received D's on my next six tests, my concentration was so off. I went from a B student to a C student and ended up passing the class with an overall grade of C. Worried about our friendship, I decided, a couple weeks later, to write her a letter, and just honestly ask what had happened and what was wrong and tell her how puzzled I was. When she answered, she apologized! For the next couple of months, we worked together at the strained relationship, and I forgave her. After a while, things really got better between Aunt Debbie and me.

On July 5, 2011, I finished my first certificate in the electronic technology class in AC/DC, and I was proud of myself because it wasn't easy. The teacher I had, Mr. Holhouser, was a great teacher, and because of him, I have a chance of doing great things in the future. However, it was during this time that I slacked off some on studying my Bible, yet my dear Lord never gave up on me, and I saw Him blessing me over and over again as time went on.

I finished my course on July 8 and got my certificate in basic electronic devices. Graduation was on August 9, 2012. What a surprise it was when college coordinator Mrs. Wolfe and Dean Mr. George Evans asked me to give the commencement speech! I never had the chance to thank them for giving me the opportunity to give the speech. I had always wanted to be a motivational speaker, and this was my opportunity to motivate. I went up to speak after Dr. Underwood, the president of Kaskaskia College.

Graduation was a great experience, and there were many important people there. We had the board of trustees from Kaskaskia College, the president and the dean of the college, many of its faculty, and our prison wardens. I was very anxious about speaking, but with God's help, I delivered what I think was a powerful speech.

When I was finished, I felt proud that I could deliver it, but I knew that it was only because Jesus had strengthened me and given me the confidence that I needed to carry through. I knew that, without Jesus in me, I would have never been able to do as well as I did, and I thanked Him for all His help.

I didn't have to dress up. I just wore a T-shirt, but I was very nervous and really perspiring, yet no one knew that I was that

Chapter 17 *Go Read*

nervous. I received a standing ovation, and members of Kaskaskia walked up to me and shook my hand. Dr. Underwood told me that he enjoyed my speech. However, you can't please everybody in prison. The white inmates told me that I sounded too black, and the black inmates told me that, if they had put a curtain in front of me, they would have sworn that I was white. Ha! I guess that means that it was just about right. There were a couple negative comments from inmates too tough for their own good, but a lot of guys said that they were moved by my speech. In the end, I was very happy about it all, and I thanked God for helping me get through it. What an experience! If only my grammar school teachers could have seen me!

My life continues to be a complete surprise since Jesus has been in my life. On August 2, 2012, I experienced a miracle that I'd wanted for a long time. I awoke that morning out of a dream. I had dreamed that my mother and I were at the lakefront in Chicago having a picnic, and we were laughing, walking, and talking, and just having a really good time. When I awoke, I felt a kind of ease come over me for her. It was a sense of peace like I'd never felt before, and at that moment, I knew that God had finally touched my heart to forgive her. My heart had been hardened toward her for many, many years, and I had not realized it until then. The anger and hatred I had carried had been such a burden. I couldn't let go of the grudge that I bore against her for letting things happen to us. How I'd wanted to let go of the bad feelings that I had had for her, to have my heart soften toward her and lift this burden off my shoulders. Now, praise God, He'd helped my feelings to come out in my dream, softening what had once been so hard. Now I felt freed from all that I'd carried through those many years. I thanked my Lord God for giving me this peace, for, not only had I freed her, but I had also freed myself! Thank You, my Lord and God – I owe you so much more than I realize!

You must know by now how much I enjoyed academic study. On April 1, 2013, I signed up for yet another class. Mrs. Wolfe wanted me to take a class called "restaurant management" for she believed it would help me with my "people skills" and make me more productive in the future. She believed that this would be a great class, and she was right! The class was by far the best vocational class I have ever had. My teacher, Mrs. Sarver, was really friendly and knew just what to do to help me notice things about myself. She especially helped me notice how much I had changed. In the class we had a guy who liked to debate and challenge everything anyone said. I personally don't like debates because I believe I have a lot more to focus on than small stuff. To combat this, I would just stop talking and let him have his point. Mrs. Sarver wanted me to learn not to let people walk over me. In reviewing my life, I feel proud of the changes I have made in not getting angry or reacting in a violent manner. I can see how I have come a long way since Jesus has been helping me let things go. However, I do understand her point. I am still learning patience and becoming more of what I'd like to be. Not a tougher man, but a better man, through the influence of the awesome people God has put in my life – people like Mrs. Sarver, who have had my best interest at heart.

Some of you may be wondering what happened to my mother, stepfather, and Jarmal. To tell you the truth, I don't know. The last I heard of Jarmal, he was living in Wisconsin with his girlfriend. Unfortunately, he was locked up for selling marijuana, and I haven't heard from him since 2002. During my entire incarceration, I never got any letters from Kathy and Yvonne, Rodent's daughters. My mother, Yolanda, and stepfather Rodent are doing all right, but I heard that they were struggling under the economy, and that was news I heard around October 2012. Whatever they are doing and wherever they are, I wish them the best, and may God bless them.

As I had not heard from some of my family in a long time, I also had not heard from Ireena in almost seven years, but I have kept praying through the years to hear from her. Around Christmas 2012, I received a Christmas card and a letter from her that she is alive and well. I was so happy to see her name on the envelope that I almost cried. I thought, *I know where my "Baby Girl" is! And she reached out to me!* How great is our God! I immediately wrote her back three letters to let her know about this "new creature in Christ," and I hoped that she would be happy to hear it.

I Am Free

Praise the Lord I am free

For I'm no longer bound

No more chains holding me

Hallelujah, I am free.

Chapter 18
I Am Free

"So if the son makes you free, you will be free indeed."

– John 8:36, NASB

On September 9, 2014, I could not sleep. I was about to be released from an institution that had been my "home" for twenty years. Apprehension robbed me of sleep and an exciting fear of the unknown heated my veins. In a few hours I was going to walk through the bars into FREEDOM! I was about to be a free man. Not only was I free *spiritually*, but I was about to be free *physically*, and I was about to walk into a world I did not know.

The next day, at 8:00 a.m., I heard my name over the loudspeaker, calling me to go to the administrative building to sign my release papers. Prison officers gave me a pair of black jogging pants and a white T-shirt to wear. After signing my release papers, they gave me an envelope that contained $13.10. Then one of the captains escorted me out of the prison. A sense of relief flooded over me. Debbie Weiland was waiting for me outside the gates in her car. She was not permitted to leave her car, so I put my belongings in the trunk of her car and got into the passenger seat. It was the first time I had ridden in a car in twenty years. The feeling was odd and puzzling. Watching the prison become smaller in the rearview mirror, I remembered thinking this day would never come. It all felt unreal.

Debbie pulled over suddenly, said a prayer, and then took a few pictures of me in front of the Centralia sign. We then drove to the home of Connie Thompson. It was just days before this that I found out that I was approved to be paroled to her home.

As Debbie drove, I felt apprehensive. Even though she was only going 30 miles per hour, it felt like 80. She wanted to take me out to eat before we went home, so we stopped at Cracker Barrel. While sitting in the restaurant, I looked over Debbie's shoulder and saw a 30/30 rifle mounted on the wall. I began to panic. I told Debbie that I was in violation of my parole since I could not be anywhere around guns. Laughing, she told me that it was considered art and that I had no need to worry. I still wanted to leave. We stayed to eat anyway, my eye occasionally glimpsing the "art piece," making sure that it was not getting any closer to me. After our nervous lunch of chicken strips and gravy, we headed to Walmart where she bought me some clothes and hygiene products. We then stopped at Kohl's where she bought church clothes for me. Lastly, we arrived at the home of Connie Thompson.

At Connie's house, I was welcomed by Grandma Shirley, Christie, Joisha, and Joisha's kids – Brian, Anthony, and Shian. They had a welcome home party for me, which caught me totally by surprise. After catching up for a while, I went to my room and then spent the evening talking with the kids. Later that evening I found out that they were moving to Florida. I felt sorry for Connie because I knew she was going to miss her grandchildren. They left at about midnight. It was difficult to sleep that night. I was accustomed to being locked in. At Connie's house, no doors or windows were locked. I kept thinking that someone would come in. I found comfort in a kitten named Scooter who spent the night in my bed. Despite my worry about the unlocked doors and windows, it was comfortable and wonderful to finally be sleeping in a bed and not on a prison mattress. The entire night I felt uneasy. I could not believe that I was a free man! Throughout the night, I kept going to the closet to try on my new clothes and shoes. At about 3:00 a.m., I went to the kitchen, got a bowl of chips and ice cream, sat on the back porch, and stuffed myself while looking up at the stars – just because I could. Scooter kept me company. Throughout the day, my constant prayer was thanks to God for freeing me and for the blessings He was pouring on me.

My first Sabbath on the outside was at Stewardson Seventh-day Adventist Church. Pastor Carlos Piña preached that day. Aunt Debbie had given me $20, and I returned my tithe out of it. A gentlemen that I met a few days before that Sabbath at Connie's gave me $200 from which I also returned tithe. Later that Sabbath, Pastor Carlos also gave me $40. I returned tithe from that as well. The first Sabbath was amazing because I met so many people who accepted me as family and did not judge or reject me because of my past. Even the kids came up and spoke to me. I met Michelle and Matt Figgins. It was so easy to talk to them. After the service, we had potluck with vegetarian food that I was not accustomed to. Though my stomach was unsettled, the day was unforgettable. Sitting and eating with Pastor Carlos and his wife, Elaine, made me feel like part of a family, and that sense of belonging was overwhelming and powerful.

After the potluck, we left for Michelle Figgin's house. I was accepted into her home as a little brother. It was surprising that she had fixed my favorite meal: spaghetti and garlic bread. We spent the remainder of the evening talking. Afterward, I returned to Connie's house. Two weeks later, I drove with Connie and Steve Thompson, Shirley and Wayne Figgins, and Christy to Three Angels Broadcasting Network for fall camp meeting. There I ran into David Butler who told me that he had arranged for me to do an interview with Dr. Yvonne Lewis and Angela Lomacang. At first I was skeptical and declined to do it. However, he convinced me that I should. Meeting people from around the world who were at camp meeting worshipping and praising God was an awesome experience. The food was exceptional but despite the wonderful time, I had to leave early to be home in time for my parole visit.

The time came when I wanted to be able to drive myself around, so Debbie and I went to the DMV so I could take the written driver's test and get a voter's registration card. I hadn't even had a chance to read the book, and I was told that I had two chances to take the test and could only miss seven questions to pass. I passed the test, missing seven questions. Debbie and Connie let me drive their cars around for a while so I could get used to driving. However, gas was expensive. Steve Thomas had a truck but told me I needed my driver's license before I could drive it. Wayne was on his way to Shelbyville, one day, and so I grabbed the opportunity to ask him if he could go with me to the DMV to get my driver's license. Without even knowing how to parallel park, I used his minivan to take the driver's test and passed.

Being in the free world and being able to support myself meant that I needed a job. I could not let anyone take care of me and hand me everything. I had an extremely difficult time finding a job because no one wanted to hire me since I had a criminal background. I put on a shirt and tie one day and went around dropping off my resume to different places. I sent in one hundred job applications but still could not land a job. This depressed me, and I began to wonder how I would fend for myself.

It was around this time that I got a call from Dr. Lewis with 3ABN, giving me the date for the interview. While I was excited, I was also nervous. Debbie was the one who took me to the studio that day, and I found out that it was for a show called Urban Report. I was becoming more and more nervous as the minutes drew closer for the interview. I was not sure whether I was ready to tell the world my story. I decided, however, that I would let God use my life as a testimony of His love. I was alive in order to declare His works. Mayri Cruz, who later became a good friend of mine, applied makeup so that the lighting would not affect my skin. Five minutes into the interview, Dr. Lewis had the cameras stop rolling because I was sweating so much. She asked for napkins but one of the crewmembers, named Bill, responded that all the napkins in America would not be enough for me. Mayri Cruz had to reapply my makeup and the interview continued.

Although I experienced some tension and nervousness, the interview was successful. After the interview, Dr. Lewis informed me that she would be working on getting me hired. God is good! I was not even expecting this, but God was already laying out the plan. We then drove over to the radio studio where I had an interview with Angela Lomacang. This time, the interview went much smoother. I was much calmer, and as we drove back home that day, I had a sense of peace. God was moving in an amazing way. There was still no positive feedback from the nearly hundred applications. However, after sometime, I received a call from Dean Probst. He was going to give me a chance to work for him on his farm. The work was tough, and I did not enjoy every day of it, but I was extremely grateful to God for the opportunity. After two months, on Christmas Eve, I got a call from Mollie Steenson offering me a job at Three Angels Broadcasting Network. It was hard to believe! God was working in an amazing way. There was still another challenge, however. I had no housing in Thompsonville, and I still needed approval from the parole agent to change locations. I prayed and wondered how I was going to find housing. One week later, Mollie Steenson called back and told me that they would provide housing for me for three months free. God is good!

On January 6, 2015, my parole agent approved for me to move to Thompsonville. I had two days to move, and on January 8 we made the trip to my new home. They were taping the program *True Knowledge of Self* when I arrived. We spoke to Dr. Lewis for a few minutes, and then headed to my new apartment where I unpacked. As the day ended and my family left, it dawned on me – I was about to live on my own! This was very different from prison. I was now responsible to cook for myself, manage money that was coming in, and spend my time wisely.

My first night was a little crazy. I ate a strawberry Nutrigrain bar, which made my lips feel like they were on fire, and I began to sweat. This was unbelievable – my first time being on my own, and I was about to end up in an emergency room from an allergic reaction to a cereal bar! I knew that Uncle Jerry and Uncle Tommy would not let me hear the end of it, and I would forever be the subject of their jokes. I sat down for a while and let the feeling pass. A few hours later, I took a hot bath, and while standing in the tub, I ate a tube of Pringles. It was amazing to be able to have my own bed to sleep in, shower when I wanted, and eat when I needed. I enjoyed those Pringles in the tub, and I ate them like that just because I could.

My work duties mainly involved editing videos for the Dare to Dream Network. I was paired with a guy named Ryan St. Hillarie who showed me the workplace and what I needed to do when it came to edit. The 3ABN staff welcomed me, and my first weeks there was a needed experience, as I began my new life of freedom in the working world. My evenings were spent driving to Rend Lake where I had the opportunity to be alone with God and share with Him all that was on my heart. The nights got lonely many times since I was on curfew and still had on my ankle monitor.

The next three months were a roller coaster for me. There were times when things were great. I was surrounded by friends and people who accepted me and cared for me. I was drawing closer to God, and I was free. Michelle paid me a visit

Chapter 18 *I Am Free*

one day with the family and gave me a surprise. They had bought me a blue Dodge Stratus! I was super excited about this. I had my own car now! I could not have been more grateful to them for this blessing, and the car was an awesome act of favor from God. Even though I got stuck in a ditch the first day I drove in the snow, it was still great.

However, there were gloomy moments as well. At times I felt discouraged and lonely. I had hours to be by myself, and boredom was a constant nuisance. Everyone around me had a family and people to retire to at the end of the day. I longed for companionship, and the curfew did not help. There were times when the other apartments on the lane were completely empty, and I would be left alone with the woods and deer as my companions. I felt as though I needed to catch up with other men my age who already had a family and life was going well for them. I had missed out on so much, and I wanted to make up for lost time. Twenty years behind bars gives you a lot of time to think about what you want your life to be like when you get out. You think of your wife and children, even though it sometimes seems impossible that that would ever become a reality. You think about the kind of home you will provide for your family and the work you will do for God. I needed to catch up! Why weren't things moving as fast for me as I wanted?

I kept forgetting to eat. For two decades, I had been on a schedule, and the guards had told me when to eat. Now that there were no guards around or people telling me when to eat, I would forget that I needed to eat. I had culinary skills but failed to put them to use. Pringles and chips became my best friends.

At work I put a lot of pressure on myself to prove to the administrators that I was capable of doing what they had hired me to do. I did not want to fail at my job, and a few times I grew impatient with myself. I wanted to do my best and excel at my job.

These were the kinds of thoughts that bombarded my mind when I was left alone. During those times, however, the Lord reminded me that He had everything under control. His timing is perfect. He gave me freedom from sin and freedom from prison. He had spared my life – many times – and He was not going to leave me now. I had to keep trusting Him with my future. I prayed a lot for guidance and wisdom. He had been with me for a long time, and I knew that He was going to keep providing, protecting, and planning.

Chapter 19
I Know You Are There

"I shall not die, but live, and declare the works
of the Lord. The Lord hath chastened me sore:
but he hath not given me over unto death."

– Psalm 118:17, 18, KJV

"Love is a plant of heavenly growth, and it
must be fostered and nourished."

– Ellen White, *Letters to Young Lovers*

"He who had been borne on a litter to Jesus rose to his
feet with the elasticity and strength of youth. The paralytic
found in Christ healing for both the soul and body."

– Ellen White, *Ministry of Healing*

On the afternoon of March 15, 2015, I was cleaning out the trunk of my car, which had gotten flooded from the rain the day before. I had heard that a volunteer, a young lady from the Caribbean, was coming to live in the apartment next to me. I had not given much thought to this visitor, but while I was cleaning my car, a van pulled up, and I assumed that the volunteer had arrived. The moment I saw her, I was afraid to get close to her. If I went too close, she would have heard how hard my heart was pounding and how difficult it was for me to swallow. She was beautiful. We were introduced by Jay Christian who had brought her, and we shook hands and our eyes met. Her name is Felecia Datus. I was captivated by this woman, her smile, her eyes. There was no going back.

Chapter 19   *I Know You Are There*

She was from the urban part of her island in the Bahamas, and she was mesmerized by the woods and the sounds of rural Illinois. As she stood there taking in the scenery, I decided to tell her my story. I did not think about how she would handle my heavy past since we were complete strangers. However, since we were going to be neighbors for two weeks, I thought it would be better for me to tell her the story rather than she hear it from someone else at work. I gave her my story in a nutshell, and her reaction blew me away. She did not even blink when I told her of my troubled childhood, my crime, and the time I had spent in prison. She was more amazed at the change that God had made in my life and wanted to know more about how I had managed to overcome the difficulties in my life. That evening I invited her to a meeting that was being held at my apartment. She politely declined, stating that she had to unpack.

About two hours later, she came and sat on the porch and stared at the stars. We spoke for a while and then retired for the night. The next few days were spent like that – work during the day, under the stars on the porch in the evening time with a friend of mine, Terrance Marshall. In attempting to fix a problem my car was having, Terrance had ended up making the situation worse. I did not mind. It gave me more time to talk to Felecia. Her love for God was evident. Her natural beauty was captivating, and her words of wisdom blew me away. God had just blessed me with her friendship and acceptance, and I was not letting go of her easily.

I was now more eager than ever to have my ankle bracelet off. It felt like an iron ball attached to my ankle, holding me down. The following Tuesday I got a call from my parole officer asking me if I had a pair of scissors with me. I thought the question was odd, but I told him that I did. He then told me that I was allowed to take off my ankle bracelet. The feeling was one of happiness and a new sense of freedom. It was a great accomplishment for me, and I knew that I had to let Felecia cut it off for me.

Within the two weeks that we had spent together, we had learned a lot about each other – enough to know that we would pursue something even after she returned home. I did not see time as on my side. I had to learn that things do not happen as quickly as I might want. In prison I dreamed of what it would be like to find a God-fearing woman and build a relationship with her. I wanted to move quickly. Felecia wanted time. We had our similarities, yet we also saw things differently, as with every other couple. She wanted time to return home and introduce me to her parents. I admired her because, while there were other women I was interested in who had run in the other direction because of my past, she decided to walk alongside me.

Over the couple of weeks after she left, we continued to spend time over Skype. She was not moving as fast as I wanted, but I was trusting in God's timing. Many would think that we moved quickly in establishing a relationship, but support was also given by those who knew and loved us both. God had worked in an extraordinary way. She had originally planned to come to volunteer in December. Had that been the case, I never would have met her. During the time after we met, we read *Letters to Young Lovers*, by Ellen White, and *Adventist Home* and *Ministry of Healing* after that. This was an answered prayer. I wanted a woman who could sit and study the Bible with me and read Ellen White books with me, and now that very desire was playing out in my life. We grew during a few short weeks. We had our challenges; however, with prayer, understanding, and forgiveness, we continued to press on.

The devil never lets up though. He will continue to find a way to destroy those who are sincerely seeking after God. He tried to destroy me in the darkest side of my family home, the darkest side of Chicago, the darkest side of a prison, but now he was about to attack me in the darkest side of my own mind.

On Sabbath morning, April 18, I was preparing for church. For some strange reason, I found it more important to sit on my sofa and debate with myself what I was going to do after the service was over that day. I did not want to be alone. I had been texting Felecia that morning, and she had encouraged me to head to church. I went to the bathroom to finish getting ready. While in the bathroom, I slipped on some water that had splashed from the sink. I fell, hit my head, and was knocked out. I wasn't sure how much time had passed, but when I came to, my head was throbbing. I grabbed the doorknob and pulled myself up. I suddenly got dizzy and fell again. This time, I hit the side of my neck and head and was out again. The second time I woke up, something felt strangely wrong. I could not move my left leg or left arm. The left side of my face felt numb.

I grabbed onto the doorknob again and attempted to stand in vain. During this time, I was thinking about the story where Jesus spoke to the paralytic and bid him take up his bed and walk. I figured that, if I continued to have faith in God, I would be able to walk again. I fell a few times more, and, finally, I could not take it anymore. I crawled out of the bathroom and into the kitchen. I tried again to get up but fell against the stove. I was terrified. I felt so helpless and hopeless. I could not believe that this was happening to me. I could not move the left side of my body, I could not call for help, and I was unable to go to the bathroom so I had to wet myself where I lay.

I was a grown thirty-five year old man with so many hopes and dreams for the future. I kept thinking about the woman I had just met a month before, whom I was sure God wanted me to be with. Yet, now I could not stand up. I kept praying that God would help me get up or send me help, but as darkness fell that Saturday night, no one came. My phone kept buzzing and ringing. I knew Felecia was trying to call me, and I tried to get to it on the couch where I had left it. I managed to get to it and notice that Felecia was texting me. The letters were jumbled, and I thought I had forgotten how to read. Then the light was extremely bright and gave me a severe headache. I passed out again and was out for the night, soaked in my own urine.

Chapter 19 *I Know You Are There*

Sunday morning I was still on the floor. When I woke up, my face was buried in the carpet that was drenched in my urine. At this point I was extremely desperate and thought that, at any moment, I would die. Suppose the trailer caught fire? What if I fell asleep and did not wake up again? How would they tell my spiritual family? How would my new girlfriend handle it? I questioned God and asked Him why so many bad things had to happen to me. Every time something has started to go right in my life or anytime I have begun to feel happiness, some tragedy has come and threatened to destroy me. This feeling was worse than prison. There was a time when I was a prisoner in a building; now I was a prisoner in my own body. I wanted to move, but I could not. My mind wanted my body to do something, yet my limbs were not cooperating. Once again, I was a prisoner.

I didn't think about eating. I only thought about not dying on the floor. I knew Felecia would not handle it well at all. She would be crushed. This love was new, and now it seemed as if it was about to end with my sudden death. I could not let that happen.

Sometime in the afternoon, I heard knocking at the glass door. Ryan my coworker was peering in at me and asking me to open the door. I told him I could not move. I watched him run back to his truck, and my thought was, *No, please don't leave me. I don't want to be alone.* He came back with a key, opened the door, and knelt over me, asking what I wanted him to do. I told him that I had been on the floor since Saturday morning and that I wanted to get into the shower. I had wet myself several times, and although I knew something was terribly wrong, I did not want to go to the hospital smelling the way I did. I was embarrassed. I was a grown man and had suddenly become so helpless. I didn't want anyone seeing or smelling how helpless I was.

Ryan would not hear it. He called the paramedics and told them that he thought I had suffered a stroke since I was paralyzed on my left side and my speech was slurred. He then called Dr. Yvonne and told her that I had just had a stroke. Instantly, I heard cars pulling up. I began to wonder how it was that for thirty hours I could not get one person to come to my aid, and then suddenly everyone came at once. I was relieved. I felt safe and knew that everything would be OK. I kept thinking about Felecia and Janelle Owens. One of my friends and coworkers told me that they would call her to let her know.

The paramedics arrived, and I was taken to Herrin Hospital. Everyone was there praying for me and giving their support. They confirmed that I did, in fact, have a stroke, and I was going to be transported to Barnes-Jewish Hospital in St. Louis. I was heading out of state. I was sure the parole board would be interested in hearing this!

I spoke to Felecia, and hearing her voice brought so much hope. Even though she was twelve hundred miles away, hearing her voice made it seem as if she was right there. God had spared my life, but it was only later that I found out that He had used Felecia.

Felecia's Side of the Story

Church had ended, and I took out my phone to sent Brian a message. Since he was an hour behind, I decided to wait because I did not want to disturb him during church. About two hours later, I sent him a photo of what I was having for Sabbath lunch. My friend Benita and I were having a good time, and I wanted to share it with him. Sometime had passed when it struck me that he had not responded. Brian was quick to answer his messages. I called him, and he still did not pick up. I let two hours pass before I tried again, and still I got no response. By the time night had come, I still had not heard from him. I thought that maybe he was upset with me. The evening before we had had a disagreement over my decision to go off to school. He was not opposed to education; however, he wanted us to be together in the same place. I thought that maybe he wanted some time alone. This seemed strange to me though.

Despite knowing him for only a few weeks, I knew that his moments of purposeful solitude did not last very long. He did not like to be alone for a very long time, so I knew he was not intentionally avoiding me. I called Aunt Debbie, his ma, and she had not heard from him that day. I think I called Uncle Jerry, who also had not heard from him, but he assumed that he was being a typical guy.

By the time I was getting ready for bed, I was worried and began to really wonder about what I could have possibly done wrong. As I was texting him, I noticed that he was online and seeing my messages. I wondered why he would not answer my messages, so I called him again, and he still did not answer. I then thought that maybe someone had stolen his phone. I ruled that out, however, since I knew that if that were the case, he would have found some other way to let me know that he did not have his phone. I went to bed but set my alarm to call him in the middle of the night and force him to answer. That did not work either. He still was not answering.

Sunday morning I was in a panic. This time my messages were not going through at all. I thought that maybe he had violated his parole and was back in prison. I went on the Illinois Department of Corrections website to check his status and saw that it had not changed; he was not incarcerated. While this was a relief, it still was not total relief because I still had no clue as to where he was. I called Uncle Jerry again, and he still had not heard from him. I called his friend Jason Bradley but hung up for fear that people might think I was a little weird for calling around when I had not heard from him for just one day. My fears were growing as the morning turned to afternoon. I called a few more of his friends, his office, and sent a Facebook message to Janelle, telling her that I was worried because I had not heard from Brian since the day before.

I began to cry. At this point I was desperate and knew that something was not right. Brian would not ignore me for this long – even if I had upset him. I cried because I knew something was wrong, but I felt helpless. I went to the church board meeting that afternoon and took his book

Chapter 19 *I Know You Are There*

manuscript with me. He was about to have it published but wanted me to read the raw version. During the meeting I saw that Mayri was calling me. I ran out of the meeting and heard only a few words: "Brian, stroke, found on floor."

Everything suddenly became a daze. It was like being thrown off a fast moving train and trying to figure out what just happened. My mind went blank. Nothing and no one else existed in my world. I was thinking one thing: when does the next plane leave? I called for my friend Benita and started to cry. I waited for the meeting to be over and headed straight home and booked the next flight out. I was allowed to speak to him, but I did not speak to him very long. Hearing his difficulty in speaking shattered my heart. His voice trembled, and I wanted to keep my spirits up for him. I told him that I was on my way.

As I walked through the airport the next day, I was calm. I knew that God was in control and that He would strengthen me. I must mention that I had been praying two prayers for a while. Before I visited 3ABN, I prayed that God would completely and drastically change my life. I did not have a clue how I wanted my life to be changed, but I knew that I did not want to be the same person after I came home from 3ABN. I also prayed that my relationship and marriage might be a ministry, a God-written love story through which many people would be inspired and saved. At this point, I was convinced that God had answered both prayers through Brian.

The flights kept getting delayed, and I really wished I could take control of the plane and head straight to St. Louis myself. I was growing impatient and needed to see Brian. As I walked through the terminal late that Monday night, I could not believe the circumstance that had brought me back so suddenly. Brian, the man I had just fallen in love with and was head over heels for, had suffered a stroke and was paralyzed. Uncle Jerry picked me up, and we headed straight to the hospital. The beeping of the machines and the sanitized air of the hospital numbed me enough to stop me from crying when I saw the man I last saw standing and waving goodbye to me now laying in a hospital bed with an IV in his arm in a seemingly troubled sleep.

I woke him with a light kiss on his cheek. We talked for a while, although I could not understand much of what he was saying because of his slurred speech. After assuring him that I would be back in the morning, I left just in time to cry while his Aunt Jackie hugged me. I spent that night doing more crying and praying than sleeping. I kept thinking how he was so close to death and could have possibly died had God not shown mercy. I cried thinking about how he had been all alone for thirty hours on the floor. I cried because my prayer for a drastically changed life had been answered – and I did not regret praying that prayer.

The stroke did not deter me from wanting Brian in my life. He was a blessing and an answered prayer. His determination, ability to be light-hearted and humorous in a tough situation, and buddy-like view of God had captivated me.

His vision for life, and his eagerness to seize life's opportunities presented an adventure. Our love, though young and fresh, was like a tender and delicate flower being threatened by a hurricane. Our root was God who had planted us. We knew we would make it because of His grace.

I kept recalling the two short weeks that had sealed us. During the evenings we had sat on the porch across from the woods, staring up at the stars and speaking of God's wonders, our lives, and our dreams. He was an excellent cook, and during the time I had been there, he had treated me to his cooking several times. My first Friday there, he had taken me to Cedar Hurst where we walked through the woods and spoke about our lives. Rend Lake and Thai D became two favorite spots for us. We had spent Sabbath afternoons with friends from church, and my last Sabbath there I had met his Uncle Jerry and Aunt Jackie. Brian had planned a surprise for every day that I was there.

I knew his life story and now saw him at one of his lowest points. I knew that our journey would have rough paths, but I also knew that, what God calls you to, He will bring you through. Seeing God's hand in Brian's life boosted my faith in Him, and while we both have much growing to do, I am confident that the Lord will never forsake His own. Being his girlfriend and loving him through his weak moments is an honor and a blessing. There were times that I cried and released my emotions, but never did I regret meeting him. I had my fears that, during the night, I would get a call saying that he had taken a turn for the worse. Whenever I left his hospital room to go outside, I feared that, when I returned, I would see doctors and nurses rushing to his side. God has an awesome way, however, of stilling our troubled hearts and calming our nerves, if only we allow Him.

I helped him memorize Psalm 118:17, 18: "I shall not die, but live, and declare the works of the Lord. The Lord hath chastened me sore: but he hath not given me over unto death" (KJV). This scripture brought much hope and comfort to us both. As the days went by and his health improved, we saw God's hand working in a marvelous way. His speech cleared up, and he only slurred when he was really tired or sleepy. He began to move his left leg and the droop on the left side of his face slowly went away. God is indeed awesome!

> In the words of Robert Frost, "The woods are lovely, dark and deep but we have promises to keep and miles to go before we sleep ... miles to go before we sleep."

Brian Speaks

According to the doctors, the first fall caused bleeding in my brain. The second fall severed an artery in my neck that led to the stroke in the right side of my brain. I was sensitive to light and kept my right eye closed the first day at the hospital. I started yawning excessively, and all I wanted to do was sleep. I became tired quickly over the simplest activity.

I developed a fear of sleeping. I was afraid to die alone, and when Felecia left the hospital each night, the fear crawled in with the darkness. Yet, in the darkness, God was there. The enemy wants to create doubt in our minds. He wants us to doubt the love and presence of God. When we give in to these doubts, we stop trusting in God and begin to trust self in order to deal with whatever problem or issue we are facing. The moment we do this, we take our eyes off Christ and we sink like Peter. Thank God for His saving grace and mercy that pulled me up time and time again from a sea of despair. The fear of sleep did not go away immediately but God was strengthening me as the days went by.

It was hard to cope with the reality that I could not walk or even sit up on my own. During that first week, Felecia had to help me through many things: feeding, exercising my paralyzed limbs, praying, and reading God's Word. My 3ABN family cheered me with their presence, and my own spiritual family gave me encouragement. Ma was sick during this time, and although it grieved her, she was unable to visit me since I would be at risk of catching what she had.

My strength returned quickly. The Thursday following the stroke, I was moved to the Rehabilitation Institute of St. Louis where I began to learn to walk again. The emotional roller coaster continued to take me for spins, but God had it all under control. At the time of this chapter, I am in a wheel chair and the woman and people I love are miles away, but God, as always, is still here.

I have questioned God as to why so much had to happen to me, but I keep remembering Job. God is greater than all of our circumstances, and as long as we continue to trust Him, one day it will all be made clear. My life was spared in order to testify of God's goodness, and I believe that He will grant me a complete recovery for His own name's sake.

God truly is in the darkest side of Chicago. There are as many versions of this darkness as there are people, but whenever you find yourself in the valley of the shadow of death, God is there!

This Fire Within Me

At the rise of the sun, **This Fire Within Me** has abruptly awakened my
   weary soul. I arise with resentment, some anger, and with no confidence
   to commence another unfortunate day in the devil's playground.

This Fire Within Me neglects my intention and desire to sojourn
   into dreams of fables; to allow my unconscious mind to be
   illusive and lavishing, with no ability to control the dream world,
   but at times where my heart can be at absolute peace.

This Fire Within Me does not comply to my demands, my sleep
   desires; it is stubborn to my laziness and forbids my return
   regardless of how I feel to be awakened. This **Fire** has graciously
   moved me to get up and out at last to see another day.

This Fire Within Me is like a sleeping giant that no one dared
   to awaken. It is a ravishing volcano that soon is about to erupt.
   This **Fire** was lying dormant in the abyss of darkness as a
   small flame, awaiting the precise moment to flourish into a
   mighty flame that will illuminate any bottomless pit.

This Fire Within Me is the steady, pulsating beat of my heart, the air that
   I inhale, and the fuel to my soul. It provides and sustains my energy; it
   permits me to perform, achieve, obtain, manage, and control my daily tasks.

This Fire Within Me allows me to overthrow any obstacle and obstruction
   in my path; to overlook any malice or envy that gives visibility to my view;
   to be insensitive toward any hatred or anger my enemies have for me.

This Fire Within Me has complete dominion over all my emotions; it subdues my tears and sorrows; it takes away my sufferings and discomforts; it restrains my enmity and hostility. It allows me to be ecstatic and rejoice; it gives me enjoyment and comfort; and it lets me show affection and tenderness. It is the reason of my awaking, the smile on my face, the joy of my day, and the life that I now live.

This Fire Within Me is like what King Solomon said: "Love flashes like **Fire,** the brightest kind of flame" (Song of Solomon 8:6). The Prophet Isaiah said, "Behold all ye that kindle a **Fire** that compass yourselves about with sparks: walk in the light of your **Fire** and in the sparks that ye have kindled" (Isaiah 50:11). So who is the awesome God who is willing to put a match to a doused heart just so I can live out His purpose by igniting this **Fire** to my heart? I was not aware that I would be engulfed by it or receive a lifetime of it.

This Fire Within Me does not fail, disappoint or collapse, but is successful, brings hope, and can build mansions under the sea. It cannot be smothered by white sand or extinguished with purified water. It is not uncertain or delicate, but strong and firm. It is a burning, blazing satisfaction and enjoyment. It is an eternal flame of love that was instilled by **God,** ignited by **Jesus,** and flourished by the **Holy Spirit.**

– Brian T. Heath

We invite you to view the complete
selection of titles we publish at:

www.TEACHServices.com

scan with your mobile
device to go directly
to our website

Please write or email us your praises, reactions, or
thoughts about this or any other book we publish at:

P.O. Box 954
Ringgold, GA 30736

Info@TEACHServices.com

TEACH Services, Inc., titles may be purchased in bulk for
educational, business, fund-raising, or sales promotional use.
For information, please e-mail:

BulkSales@TEACHServices.com

Finally if you are interested in seeing
your own book in print, please contact us at

publishing@TEACHServices.com

We would be happy to review your manuscript for free.

www.ingramcontent.com/pod-product-compliance
Lightning Source LLC
Chambersburg PA
CBHW081840170426
43199CB00017B/2795